FABRICE GUÉROUX

REAL & FAKE WATCHES

Handbook on watch counterfeits

watchprint.com
publications on jewellery and watches

This book is not an official book and has not been approved by the brands that are mentioned. It was created for information purposes only and is intended to help you recognise counterfeits.

PHOTO CREDITS :
Part 3 - comparisons between original watches and counterfeits
Original watch photos: © 2009 – MMC – www.montres-modernes.com
Sincere thanks to Olivier Fort for the loan of the counterfeit
Rolex moon-phase model.

Special thanks to Michel Arnoux and the team of the Federation of the Swiss Watch Industry for their valuable help, for the photos of fake watches in chapter 4 "Counterfeits and the future of fakes", as well as the photos of watch dials.

TRANSLATION :
Susan Jaquet, Transcribe (Timely English)

ISBN: 978-2-9700656-3-0

Foreword

Forgery and the use of forgery - by Stephan Ciejka

The struggle against counterfeits is a war that is waged daily against a formidable enemy. Flexible and efficient, it constantly adapts to new developments, and its pitiful front – often a street seller who inspires more pity than contempt – conceals a set of incredibly professional networks. The fake objects seized by specialized services such as police or customs are produced by the million, thereby depriving companies of a substantial portion of their legitimate income, and the community of the various taxes and duties that contribute to running state-operated services. The chief beneficiaries are instead mafia-run cartels and the underground economy.
While it is especially important that brands should join forces in defending their creations, either directly or through institutions such as the Fondation de la Haute Horlogerie and the Federation of the Swiss Watch Industry, it is also up to everyone, including consumers and political leaders, to become aware of the wealth produced by luxury industries – both from a strictly financial standpoint and in terms of the jobs it generates in Europe.
For many years now, Fabrice Guéroux has been actively involved in this struggle which, while undoubtedly an unequal battle, is one in which individual initiatives may prove at least as effective as the often cumbersome measures taken by certain institutions. His contribution lies in creating an encyclopaedia of fake watches. Rather than making declarations of intent, he prefers to show, to inform, to describe and to explain. In this book, he meticulously dissects the mechanism of counterfeiting in all its forms, whether basic or sophisticated. He demonstrates, for example, that forgerers and counterfeiters, be they talented artisans or neo-industrialists, share with their customers – which might mean you if you're not careful – the same status as delinquents. Fakes are not chic, but they also stand for theft.

Stephan Ciejka is one of the leading international wristwatch specialists. A journalist and reporter, he is currently editor-in-chief of the oldest French-language trade magazine, the monthly Revue des Montres.

About this book

The first edition of "Real and Fake Watches" was published in 2006. There is still no similar book on the topic, which presents an introduction to the controversial field of counterfeits along with precise comparisons on 13 brands and more than 85 models.

The first edition is still valid for certain models, but in view of the market evolution and demand, many of these models have evolved and we are now unfortunately facing a major problem: that of the race to achieve quality.

The author has also evolved over the past three years, and that is why he wished to update this edition and to present a brand-new book presenting this evolution.

A number of seasoned connoisseurs or watch experts will enjoy focusing on such or such a legal or technical detail. This book is intended for everyone. Experts and connoisseurs will probably find information to complement their existing knowledge, and the author will be delighted to receive their comments. The comments received over the past three years have made a substantial contribution to improving this new book.

In this edition, enthusiasts will discover the world of counterfeits and a whole host of information and illustrations that will help them to recognize a counterfeit and become more professional in their approach to the world of watchmaking.

This book is different from the first one in that readers will not find detailed comparisons. The pursuit of quality over the past two years has made it impossible to provide stable comparisons between original and counterfeit watches. You might see a difference today between a real Rolex and a fake Rolex, such as on the hands, and in four months' time that difference will have vanished. The author has thus taken an entirely different approach and is therefore offering you a far more richly illustrated book than the first in terms of both brands and models. Readers will thus be able to see for themselves the most common differences, and it is the sum of all these observations that will enable them to identify a watch during a purchase. After reading through the book several times, the excitement of an impulse purchase, by far the greatest trap for a buyer, will perhaps have died out and been replaced by a wiser, more cautious attitude.

It is important to remember that counterfeiting is a criminal activity. What's the difference between this activity and drug, weapons or human trafficking? Only the risks in terms of criminal penalties! Getting caught with a dozen fake watches during a customs control will at worst cost you a month-long prison sentence. Getting arrested with 50 grams of cocaine is an entirely different matter – and that's the only difference. As far as the rest is concerned, it's a criminal activity just like any other, representing phenomenal sales figures and based on the exploitation of thousands of people. It's an activity that serves to launder money for the world's most powerful criminal organizations, many of which are involved in all kinds of activities, from drug trafficking to arms trafficking, from money-laundering to the sale of personal banking information.
The author's aim is to raise public awareness and help people realize what market they are taking part in if they buy fakes.

This book does not claim to provide comprehensive knowledge on the topic, but will undoubtedly provide everyone with certain answers to the questions they have on counterfeit watches.

The Publisher

CONTENTS

About the author

The success of the first work and demand for a second volume have led me to pursue my research in the field of fake watches. We are unfortunately seeing that the constant demand for luxury products, along with the considerable opportunities provided by the internet, now enable counterfeiters to distribute their "watches" almost as easily as any other product.

When the first volume of "Real and Fake watches" was published (in French only), the manufacturing quality of fake watches was far inferior to current standards and the number of watches affected by this scourge amounted to only 20 to 30% of what we now find on the market. These days, the watch has become a cult object, but the massive influx of fakes is having a detrimental effect on this ever-increasing passion for horology. Internet frauds have reached new peaks over the past two years and it is truly time to raise awareness among consumers, be they connoisseurs or novices.

This is exactly what I have taken time to address and I sincerely hope that this second book will satisfy those who purchased the first volume of "Real & Fake watches" as well as new enthusiasts.

I wish to thank Eric Hamdi, Stephan Cijeka and Michel Arnoux for their help and for believing in the usefulness of this work, along with the team of the Fondation de la Haute Horlogerie. All these individuals consistently show great generosity in sharing their passion for watchmaking.

Fabrice Guéroux

Part 1

Introduction to counterfeits

- **Counterfeits, an expanding market**
- **Contemporary watches: the core market**
- **Collector's watches: dangerous territory!**

Counterfeit: *imitate with intent to deceive; a false or spurious imitation; something not genuine*
Oxford English Dictionary

Counterfeits, an expanding market

The watch industry is in a complete spin. Coping with the economic crisis that struck in 2009 while simultaneously trying to jugulate watch counterfeits, a growing and ever more threatening scourge, has been a real challenge. It is a complicated struggle that now affects the entire watch industry.

A lot of ink has been spilt in recent years on this topic and brands have developed and implemented a number of strategies to fight this scourge. Nonetheless, last year's statistics on the sale of counterfeits appear to show that these measures have not achieved the desired results.

Who hasn't received e-mail adverts over the past two years offering branded watches for less than 300 euros? In 2008 and 2009, the internet reached new heights in terms of furthering the work of counterfeiters. Spam mail is just one example. On a different level, despite its counterfeit alert campaign, eBay has provided the means for a number of fraudulent sellers to palm off their products, often via advertisers presenting their products as "not counterfeit" or as "replicas"... As for Google, the world's number one search engine, it displayed a huge number of fake watch sites in 2008 and 2009 via its commercial links known as "adwords" – not to mention the fraudulent sites that appear on the first page after keyword searches such as Rolex, Breitling or Panerai!

Does the problem of counterfeits only concern watch brands and a handful of associations involved in the anti-counterfeit struggle? The annihilation of the fake industry is a far more complex problem than it might appear, in that the profits it generates over and above its own sales figures represent a factor that tends to dampen enthusiasm for the fight itself.

In 2009, we entered a crisis period and watch industry profits went into a decline. This is a time for saving money and new strategies have thus emerged within one of the most severely affected industries: that of *haute horlogerie*, or fine watchmaking. While the crisis is having a negative effect on the watch market, and indeed on other markets, it may well be having just the opposite effect on the popularity of counterfeits, by increasing the number of buyers liable to flirt with this market. We can therefore expect to see an increasing flow of communication and production from the makers of fake watches, as well as an increase in public demand. After all, the fact that revenues of genuine producers are going to stagnate or even fall suggests that consumer demand will also drop dramatically.

An ambitious strategy for a wide-scale struggle

In order to fully grasp the current context, it has to be viewed from all angles: the economic problem caused by counterfeits will have repercussions both on the manufacturers themselves and on consumers. What will happen to our passion for watches if manufacturers have no other choice but to close down amid a flood of cheap products imitating their own products and displaying a level of quality so similar that it's hard to tell them apart? The struggle is fierce on this front too. While watch manufacturers are progressing rapidly in their pursuit of quality while ensuring respect for traditions, counterfeiters are also upping the pace and their products currently on the market are capable of deceiving a number of amateurs... and even professionals. If you have to become a seasoned expert to know how to buy a watch online, you might as well just give up right away.

Nor should we forget that many brands suffered a great deal during the period when quartz movements first hit the market. Does that mean it's just a question of market laws? The answer is yes as far as the invasion of quartz watches in the 1970s and early 1980s is concerned. But it's definitely "no" in relation to the expansion of counterfeits since the internet became readily accessible to the public at large. The latter phenomenon is not a question of competition, for we are dealing with criminal organizations and the considerable communications means they now have for promoting their products.

What can be done within such a context? Leave the fine watchmaking industry to fight its own battle? No, because it will soon be out of its depth. While its progress is being hampered by administrative red tape, the counterfeit industry is moving ahead at top speed.

Each of us must examine the problem in order to evaluate the long-term consequences. If we wish to preserve this watch industry that we so deeply cherish and which had enjoyed spectacular recent expansion after years of stagnation, we need to make a personal commitment to saying "no to fakes".

A. LANGE & SÖHNE
GLASHÜTTE I/SA
31
AUF
AB
TOURBILLON
MADE IN GERMANY
DOPPELFEDERHAUS
FAKE

Contemporary watches: the core market

There are many angles of attack. Whereas 10 years ago the kind of fakes that might take in consumers could generally be found on tourist markets, things are very different now. The internet has become the main source of business for counterfeiters and this state of affairs is likely to worsen in the aftermath of the latest economic crisis.
While this economic crisis is continuing to have a negative impact on watch sales figures, one can safely bet that it will have the opposite effect on the sale of fake products.

Consumers' reluctance to spend money tends to increase demand for counterfeits, which is constantly activated by marketing professionals who are never short of arguments. Not to mention the influence of celebrity magazines that are capable of generating instant strong demand for a given product. So yes, the counterfeit market can undoubtedly look forward to a bright future unless effective techniques are developed to wipe it out.

The market currently most severely affected is, of course, that of contemporary watches. Witness the fact that some fake models are sold even before the genuine originals hit the retail market.
To say that the crisis is untimely is a euphemism, particularly in light of the unprecedented expansion enjoyed by the Swiss watch industry in recent years.

Counterfeiting can be summed up in figures. Sales generated by the sale of fake products are estimated at one billion Swiss francs corresponding to 40 million watches, compared with 26 million original watches. (source: Federation of the Swiss Watch Industry – FH).
Asia alone accounts for 80% of production. The means employed for both production and distribution are certainly clever, ranging from simply dispatching a fake watch via a standard express courier, or even a traditional postal service; to a massive influx of fake watch products via maritime freight sent to distributing countries.

Watch counterfeits can be viewed from two different angles: the manufacturing quality as such and its repercussions on demand from various potential buyers in terms of brands; and the damage viewed as a whole.

In terms of quality, the market offers an extremely broad range of products, from "ultra-cheap" watches to chronographs equipped with a Valjoux 7750 movement or even an almost identical copy of the original, equipped with a power reserve and a fully functional perpetual calendar. Soon, we can even expect to see functional tourbillons on fakes sold for under 1,000 euros.

Criminal activity with disastrous consequences

In economic terms, the loss of earnings directly affects retailers and manufacturers, even though a large number of counterfeit buyers are not potential customers of the fine watchmaking industry. It would thus be wrong to consider that the millions of euros generated by counterfeits are all income lost to the watch industry.

The real issue arising from the counterfeiting of contemporary watches is its impact on brand image, a vicious spiral with potentially disastrous economic consequences. Let's take a look at the repercussions of this criminal activity on the watch industry. The strength of a brand and the guarantee of its longevity and its reputation stem specifically from its brand image, chiefly characterized by the manner in which it is perceived by the public. All you need do to is to ask an average consumer "What is a Rolex for you?" and you'll inevitably get the following type of response: "a luxury watch brand", "the best-known luxury watch brand".
The press in certain European countries has certainly done enough to promote this image in recent months. The brand will be systematically associated with luxury products and quality. But what about this brand image if the first question people ask when they see your new

diver's watch becomes "Is it a fake?". That would prove that not only have counterfeits been gaining ground, but they also damage the hard-earned brand image.

Counterfeiting contemporary watches therefore definitely has an extremely negative impact on the watch industry and on its brand image. It is also increasingly detrimental to its future. When your entourage no longer worries about checking whether you are wearing a real or a fake watch, because they simply can't be bothered, that will mean the end of the art of fine watchmaking. It will no longer have any place within an impersonal society that is swamped by the over-consumption of disposable products. Exactly like a rapidly spreading virus, the counterfeit market is no longer content with contaminating contemporary watches alone, but is also affecting collector's watches to a truly alarming extent.

ROLEX
GMT-MASTER
SUPERLATIVE CHRONOMETER
OFFICIALLY CERTIFIED
SWISS

FAKE

Collector's watches: dangerous territory

Counterfeits are not inevitable. While we are currently suffering from this plague, we have to grasp the fact that it didn't get here by chance. Nor is the collector's market immune from it.
Although completely different from the counterfeiting of contemporary watches, that of collector's watches is nonetheless extremely dangerous for brands. Before becoming brand "aficionados", many of us first tried our luck with collectors' or vintage watches.
Over the past 10 years, the collector's watch market has grown to an extent that even the most specialized observers among us could not have imagined 20 years ago. The records regularly reached in auction rooms speak for themselves.

A "Rolex Submariner" which used to sell for a little under 2,500 euros has more than doubled its auction value within five years. Contrary to the claims of certain big-name brands, this market is important, and an increasingly large number of watch devotees are just as interested in collector's watches as in contemporary models. From the unscrupulous perspective of counterfeiters or forgerers, whether amateur or professional, this is an extremely lucrative market.

And that is exactly what we are seeing today. We are dealing with a market that is in need of a swift clean-up because of the large numbers of counterfeit players, ranging from the straightforward counterfeiter to the excellent watchmakers of South American and Eastern European countries, capable of reassembling a 1968 Omega "Speedmaster" based on parts from watches made in three different years.

Several gaps that have enabled counterfeiters to infiltrate the market are the result of severe negligence: the failure to ascertain whether such watches do indeed perpetuate authentic watchmaking traditions, to verify the quality of production (professionals such as MMC or Olivine – well-known second-hand dealers in Paris – speak of

"18/20 minimum watches") or the provenance of models; failure to make use of experienced experts, etc.
The enthusiasm for Omega, Zenith and other watches from the 1950s has reached unprecedented proportions; while 100 euros

used to be enough to buy certain models, prices now sometimes exceed 2,000 euros. There is nothing easier, for a clever watchmaker, than to get an old 1950 Omega working again using a case, a revamped mechanism, a freshly repainted dial and a standard pair of hands – and then take a nice series of photos to enhance his advert on eBay.
An eye-catching title will present it as a rare and inexpensive piece that is offered at 1,000 euros. The intention is to incite you to acquire this "unique" piece that was not made in any Omega workshop. Even worse than a straightforward counterfeit, it is also and above all a fake watch.

From counterfeiters to forgerers

Fraud can be taken to the next level by those such as Eastern European counterfeiters who have come to specialize in watches that have never existed.

They use a very simple recipe: a forgerer welds four lugs onto a pocket-watch, adds an enamelled dial by the brand of his choice (usually Vacheron Constantin, Breguet or Patek Philippe). All they need then do is add a bridge bearing the brand name to an ordinary vintage regulator-type movement, and they are all set up with a pocket-watch transformed into a large-size (52 mm) wristwatch! In such cases, there is no point in advertizing a high price on the model on the internet, a starting price of 100 euros will be enough to attract novice collectors who might end up buying it for over 3,000 euros!

Welcome to the market of repainted dials, generic hands (non-original models), fake cases, watches sold with forged papers, and all manner of other counterfeit products!
But there is worse still, since the market is full of geniuses in the area of repainted dials, which is why we are finding an increasing number of counterfeits of highly valued models. It is not unusual to find red "Rolex Submariner" watches, Comex models, rare military watches and even "Daytona Paul Newman" watches with repainted dials, hastily assembled calibres and false documents...

The internet has become one of the most popular meeting points for collector's watch enthusiasts – both buyers and sellers. It often features models offered at 20 to 30% of their real value.

That is why a number of "collectors", happy to have found an investment source so effectively promoted by the press over the past five years, end up with a Rolex or a Breguet Type XX watch that is only 30% genuine, or rather 70% fake! Moreover, they are in for a severe disappointment, since most of them will not even realize they've been taken for a ride until one or two years later when they show their model to an expert who will reveal its true nature.

In a nutshell, suspicion and caution are the order of the day. Before launching into building a collection, it's well worth learning all the tricks of the perverted trade of the counterfeiter – the most reliable manner being to rely on the well-informed advice of genuine connoisseurs.

Part 2

The varying quality of counterfeits

- **Where are they made?**
- **Counterfeits equipped with Chinese movements**
- **Counterfeits equipped with "Swiss" movements**
- **What can you expect from a copy?**
- **Levels of quality among replicas**
- **Other types of counterfeits**

Here's a first chapter in which the topic is dealt with in a fairly broad manner. It represents an initial approach to the subject and is mainly intended for novices. We will return later to more detailed aspects, particularly regarding the main type of contemporary counterfeits found on the market, and we will also look in more detail at vintage watches, collectors' watches, "genuine fakes" and forged products.
In order to distinguish between what is ostensibly offered on the fake market and what is actually there, let's look at the issue first from a beginner's standpoint.

Where are they made?

As far as the various types of counterfeits are concerned, you will probably hear talk of "Chinese", "Thai", "Japanese" and even "Swiss" copies. Let's immediately put an end to such misleading marketing: over 70% of the counterfeit market is Asian. There is no such thing as "Japanese" or "Swiss" counterfeits, as least as far as industrial production is concerned, but we will repeatedly deal with this topic throughout the book. There are however several different types of quality in the field of "replicas" (an alternative and misleading term for counterfeits).

Fake

Over a long period, websites offering counterfeits used to present replicas featuring various degrees of production quality. They were variously labelled "A quality", "Grade B" or "Grade 1". The numbered grades often ranged from 1 to 5. This approach is now quite unusual and counterfeiters hawking their products on the web have reduced the issue to presenting models with a "Chinese movement" or a "Swiss movement". The average sales price for the former type of watch is around 150 US dollars, compared with 300 US$ to 1,000 US$ for the latter category – and even more when the materials used for counterfeits are precious materials such as gold or platinum.

Counterfeits equipped with Chinese movements

These are poor-quality watches. The worst specimens are distributed on tourist markets and are intended for tourists wanting to have fun with a fake branded watch bought for less than 50 dollars. But these watches do not represent a real danger for the watch industry, in that they are mainly destined to amuse tourists and no attempt is usually made to pretend that they are anything other than fakes.

Fake

The real danger lies on the internet, in watches equipped with Chinese automatic, hand-wound or chronograph movements. That is where these days a photo is barely enough to tell the difference between a real and a fake watch – and that spells a real danger for manufacturers. First of all, it is detrimental to the brand image. How can you sell an almost identical watch for 150 US$ when the real one costs around 5,000 US$? Within the fine watch industry, the value of a watch lies chiefly in the quality of the movement and in the manufacturing quality. A poorly made fake is an object that merely resembles the original as closely as possible. And that is all counterfeiters are doing by offering poor-quality products.

A watch labelled as equipped with a "Chinese movement" is just a poor-quality fake with a dicey movement, cheap materials, shoddy finishing, etc. At best, these watches may be equipped with a Japanese movement by the Miyota brand.

Counterfeits equipped with "Swiss" movements

These models are the hardest to identify. Here again, the term "Swiss" is only a trap to snare customers. All counterfeit models produced in large quantities are made in China and the movements are fakes too – generally copies of movements by ETA (the major manufacturer of high-quality Swiss movements). Some chronographs are equipped with Poljot (Russian) movements. One of the key factors entitling a watch to be labelled a "Swiss watch" is its movement. Contrary to what many industrial-scale producers of replica watches would have us believe, there are no counterfeit production factories in Switzerland!

The problem is that counterfeiters have devoted particular attention in recent years to these "fake movements", and that it is hardly surprising to find movements boasting a quality almost identical to the real ones used by certain brands. Demand has been so strong since 2006 that Asia has invested in factories equipped with the finest machinery and high-quality materials. This is what now enables them to flood the market with watches of very good quality.

What can you expect from a copy?

This work is intended to help you avoid falling prey to a fraud, and not to help you buy a "quality" fake. Whether they are of dismal or good quality, you cannot expect anything more from such a purchase than to own a copy, and thus to be taking part in the operation of this fraudulent market.

Don't buy copies; buy yourself an affordable watch that matches your budget and will bring you genuine pleasure. The only thing you might do is buy one in order to take it apart and learn how they are made in order to distinguish them from the real ones. But to do that, you would need a real one. So don't waste your money, I've already been there and I am sharing the results of such experiences with you in this book!

The most widely copied brands

The most widely copied brands are Rolex, Panerai and Cartier, but with the strong growth in the watch market over recent years, a number of other brands are now falling victim to the same fate: Zenith, TAG Heuer, Blancpain, Breitling, etc.

Levels of quality among replicas

Before getting down to a detailed study of the various quality levels or grades, and in order to sharpen your sense of observation, I suggest you pay a visit to a large jeweller's store and take a look at various models. You will see for yourself that the high prices of luxury watches are rarely unjustified. You will be able to observe the precision with which the various parts have been crafted, to appraise the weight of a watch, admire the quality of the glass, the steel or the gold, the complexity of a movement when it's visible through the back of the watch, etc.

No counterfeit, even of good quality, will ever have the look and touch of a real one. This is true and will remain so for a long time to come, for a very simple reason: cost. Imagine the investment required to set up a factory to make counterfeits: spare parts, lathes,, watch glasses, bracelets and straps, dials, etc. The number of spare parts required and the resulting production costs are extremely high. Taking the case of a Rolex, particularly since replicas of its creations have been around for such a long time and that the original models only rarely change, a counterfeiter would need to invest at least two million euros just to make these models. So imagine the cost of a factory that could make copies of watches by most of the brands, which change quite regularly... That's a huge risk to run for an activity that is both criminal and necessarily ephemeral – although manufacturers have a tough time grasping the latter reality!

Grades of quality among counterfeits

As explained earlier, it is in fact pointless to describe counterfeits in terms of their quality, since the majority of products offered on the internet are of good and even very good quality. It is nonetheless necessary to give a detailed description of these products, for while it is very easy for some of us to recognize an average-quality watch,

things can get much more difficult in the case of certain particularly high-quality counterfeits.
To begin getting your eyes used to appraising the various degrees of quality among counterfeits, we are going to arbitrarily give them a grade ranging from 1 to 5.

1 out of 5 quality

These are very low-end quartz-driven watches. They bear little resemblance to the original models, and very few people will actually offer you them while attempting to make you believe they are real. This category of counterfeits is of no real interest and they are generally found on tourist-oriented markets, and at ridiculously cheap prices.

2 out of 5 quality

This quality of counterfeit is already harder to identify and it affects a number of brands. That being said, even if they are equipped with automatic Japanese movements, they are nonetheless poor replicas and do not deceive too many people.

3 out of 5 quality

These are the kinds of counterfeits most commonly distributed via the internet. They are equipped with movements of mediocre quality and the counterfeiters pay greater attention to the outward appearance of the watch than to the quality of its interior. The movements often do not even bear the brand name.

You will find only "Rolex" branded watches in this category. It is worth noting in this context that almost all Rolex models have been copied, including the Submariner model commemorating the model's 50th anniversary and the Deepsea!
At this stage, you'll need to begin looking carefully in order to tell a fake watch from a real one, especially when you are dealing with online sales, where the photos supplied are the only factor that will enable you to determine whether you are prepared to go ahead with the transaction. They are fairly easy to identify when it comes to models with date displays such as the Submariner, Datejust and Day-Date. But you will discover later on in this book that collectors' watches are increasingly being copied. This is because they attract higher prices at public auctions. Many of them do not have a date, and the strap or bracelet can also "say" a lot about them. On gold or gold and steel models, they have poor-quality plating which tends to wear off quite quickly, especially at the edges or where bracelet parts move against one another.

Fake

4 out of 5 quality

There are a number of lies circulating in the field of counterfeits, the first being that these watches are 99% faithful copies; and the second that these watches are made in Switzerland. As I've already said, there are no factories for counterfeits in Switzerland, even though some websites specializing in information on counterfeits may make claims to the contrary – which is basically only a means of promoting the work of the manufacturers and distributors of fakes. These watches have a self-winding ETA movement (ETA Valjoux 7750) as far as copies of the Rolex Daytona are concerned. They are extremely hard to recognize and are often sold along with a presentation box and identification papers, which are just as fake as the watch itself. The series number indicated on the paper and the case is identical and thus matches the model. Rolex replica watches also feature a green sticker under the case.

Fake

5 out of 5 quality

Authentic versions of the watches in this category are equipped with an ETA base movement. Asia now has sufficient technological means of reproducing these movements to frighteningly high production standards. While *haute horlogerie* watches equipped with complicated movements such as Vacheron Constantin or Patek Philippe models, for example, are not really affected by this realistic type of counterfeit, watches equipped with ETA base movements are far more vulnerable.

Other types of counterfeits

So-called "home-made" watches

These watches may be of extremely good quality. What I refer to as "home-made production" means watches that are modified versions of "high-quality" counterfeits. Take for example a 5/5 quality fake Rolex Submariner, and modify a certain number of details that require improvement. Some counterfeiters thereby manage to produce watches that you will not be able to identify by means of a photo, simply because they will be careful to show you only a few convincing details that are obviously similar to those of the real models: the serial number, the size of the holes for the spring-bar bracelet lugs, the 2.5X magnified date window, etc... Nor is it unusual to find fake components fitted in authentic watches. All of which goes to show one must be extremely alert and not just be content with checking one or two points.

Fake

Collectors' watch counterfeits

The collectors' watch market has been severely affected over the past three years and the quality of the counterfeits on offer has moved firmly upmarket. One need only observe the sky-high prices achieved at certain auctions to grasp why counterfeiters have decided to make a closer study of this field. Let's first consider Rolex, of which certain models such as the Red Submariner, the

James Bond (the first Submariner), the Turn-O-Graph, the Explorer (the Milgauss model or the Steve McQueen model), the Daytona Paul Newman, etc., are particularly highly sought-after. One can now find extremely high-quality replicas that have just recently arrived on the counterfeit market. Most of them are very hard to identify and it is virtually impossible to do so based on a photograph alone. Nor is Rolex the only brand affected. Recent enthusiasm for military watches means that we are also now seeing fake watches purported to be made by Omega, IWC, Lange and other brands that produced models equipping the armies of the different countries at war during the 1930s and 1940s.

Since this market is steadily growing, you are bound to come across more and more of these counterfeit models. While it might seem rather scary when you look at photographs to realize that it can prove hard to tell a fake watch from a real one and that there is a real risk of being taken for a ride, it is pretty rare not to find an infallible means of avoiding any unpleasant surprises. The first thing to do is to find out whether the model exists! As incredible as it might seem, certain watch models that simply do not exist are offered for sale. Getting information about sellers and finding out whether they are reliable is another way of sparing oneself future disappointment. But as we move on to the "practical phase", the best means of gaining confidence is to become an expert in verifying watches.

"Genuine fake watches"

These are generally originals that have been modified in order to give them value, as in the case of a standard Rolex Submariner transformed into a model that is impossible to find on the auction market, simply by adding a fake dial bearing the Comex logo or a military logo. Hence the term "genuine fake watch". An entire chapter at the end of this book is devoted to this type of counterfeit.

Fake

Comparisons between original watches and counterfeits

For practical reasons relating to keeping it up-to-date, this section will not be dealt with in detail as it was in the previous reference work. Since counterfeits evolve at an increasingly fast pace, this can mean that certain information rapidly becomes obsolete.

This section will therefore be presented in a simpler but richly illustrated manner. Its goal is to accustom readers to observing for themselves the most frequent differences between original watches and counterfeits.

The counterfeit watches shown in this section are medium or good-quality Asian watches.

Some may notice that some of the models presented are hardly worth it, given the major differences between the original and the fake. Nonetheless, they do display a relative degree of quality, and these differences tend to dwindle over time, including sometimes in the very next year after their production.

A more detailed later chapter is devoted specifically to high-quality counterfeits.

ORIGINAL DATEJUST

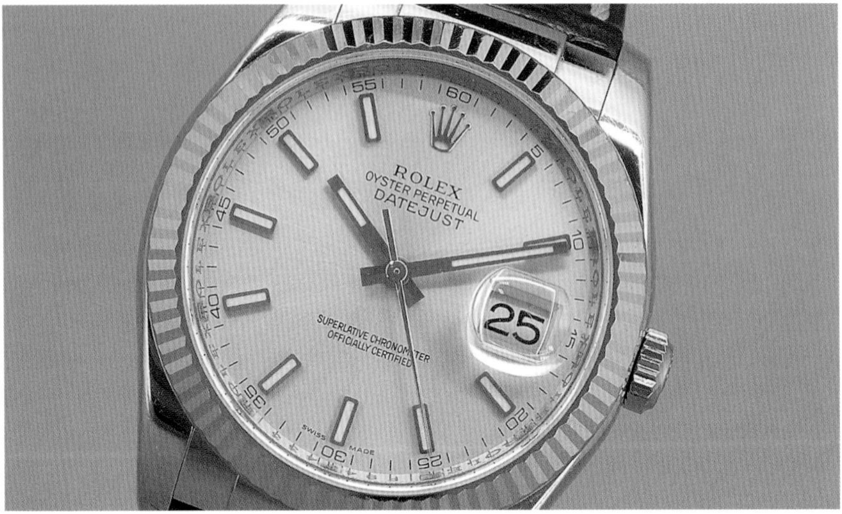

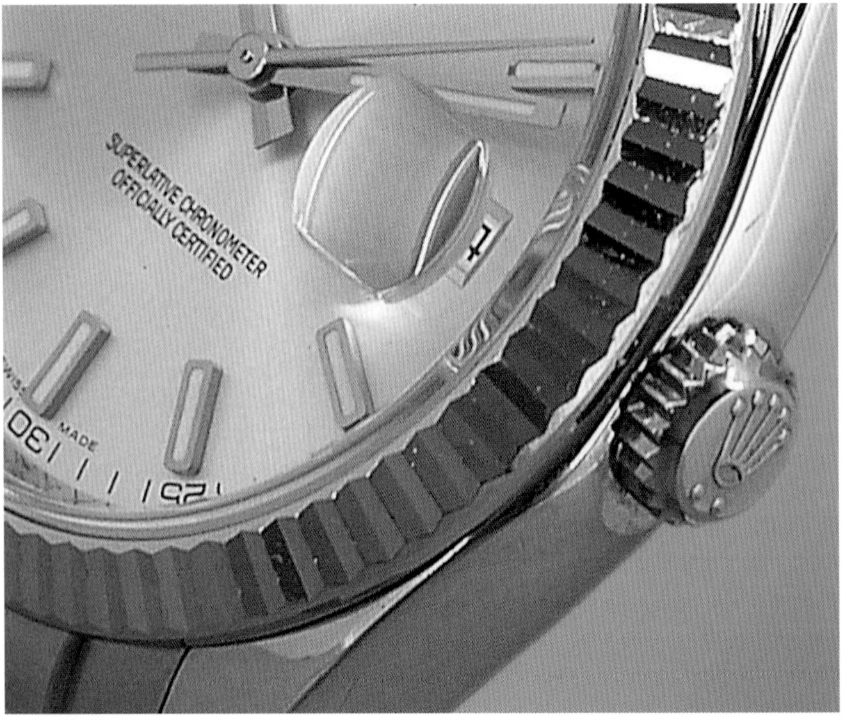

FAKE DATEJUST

MAIN DIFFERENCES: different lettering on the "Superlative Chronometer Officially Certified" marking (sans-serif font on the fake and a bold font on the original). The calibre inside is an imitation ETA movement. Double-dot winding-crown on the original for independent date and time adjustment (compared with a bar on the fake). Overall finishing (see the crown).

ORIGINAL DAY-DATE

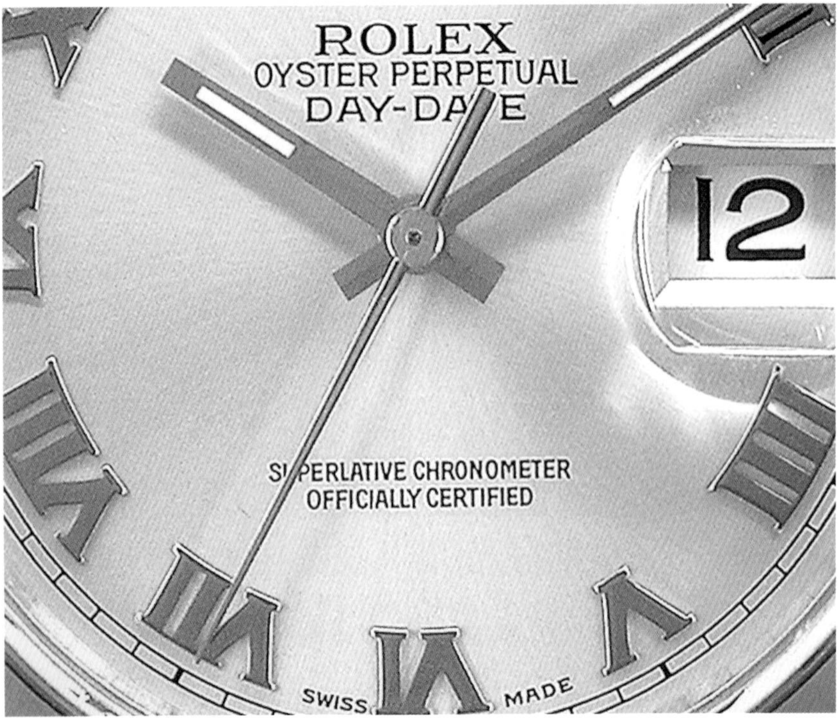

FAKE DAY-DATE

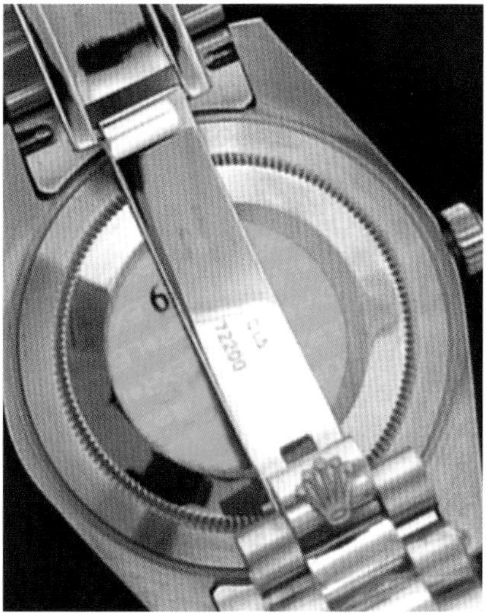

MAIN DIFFERENCES: different lettering on the "Superlative Chronometer Officially Certified" marking (sans-serif font on the fake and bold font on the original). The calibre inside is an imitation ETA movement. Double-dot winding crown on the original for independent date and time adjustment (compared with a bar on the fake). Overall finishing (see the crown).

ORIGINAL DAY-DATE

FAKE DAY-DATE

MAIN DIFFERENCES: the most blatantly obvious difference on the gold models is of course the weight of the watch; the counterfeit is substantially lighter. The calibre inside is an imitation ETA movement. Double-dot winding crown on the original for independent date and time adjustment (compared with a bar on the fake). Overall finishing (see the crown).

ORIGINAL EXPLORER I

FAKE EXPLORER I

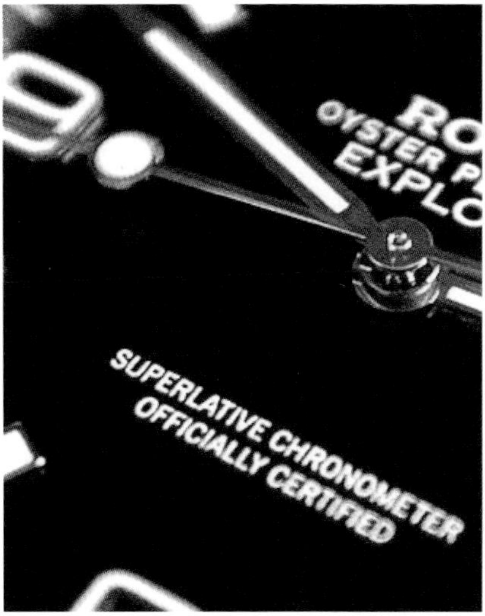

MAIN DIFFERENCES: different lettering on the "Superlative Chronometer Officially Certified" marking (sans-serif font on the fake and bold font on the original). The calibre inside is an imitation ETA movement. For a model like this one, it's essential to actually open up the watch, since the external appearance can be very deceptive. Sometimes only the movement will reveal the difference.

ORIGINAL EXPLORER II

FAKE EXPLORER II

MAIN DIFFERENCES: different lettering on the "Superlative Chronometer Officially Certified" marking (sans-serif font on the fake and bold font on the original). The calibre inside is an imitation ETA movement. For a model like this one, it's essential to actually open up the watch, since the external appearance can be very deceptive. Sometimes only the movement will reveal the difference.

ORIGINAL DAYTONA 16520

FAKE DAYTONA

MAIN DIFFERENCES: the calibre inside is an imitation ETA movement (7750). For a model like this one, it's essential to actually open up the watch, since the external appearance can be very deceptive. Sometimes only the movement will reveal the difference.

ORIGINAL DAYTONA

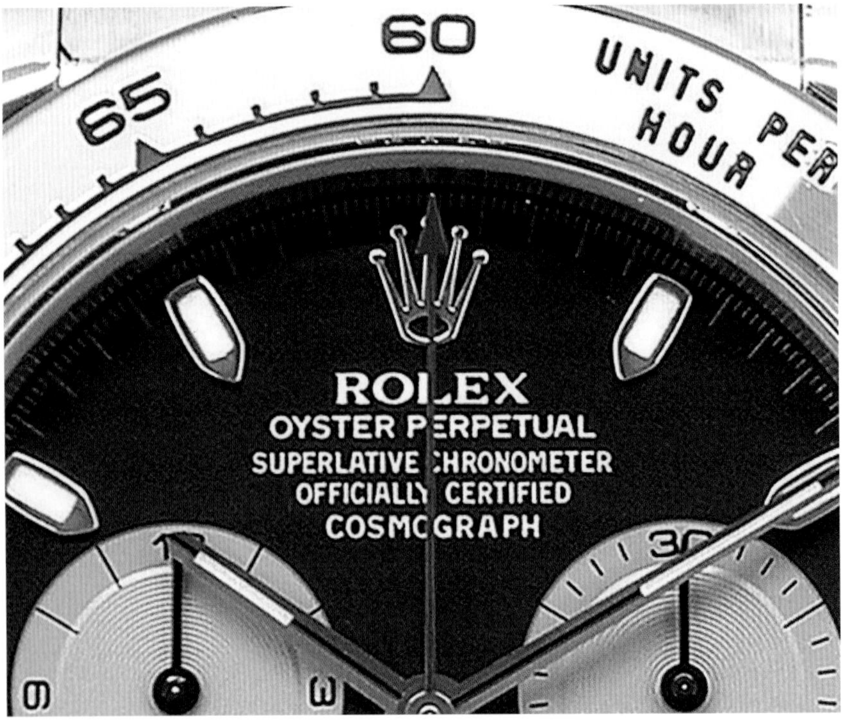

FAKE DAYTONA

MAIN DIFFERENCES: the most obvious is of course the weight of the watch (gold on the original or electroplating on the fake. The calibre inside is an imitation ETA movement (7750). Nonetheless, it's essential to open up the watch, since the external appearance can be very deceptive, especially in the case of a solid gold fake.

ORIGINAL DAYTONA 116520

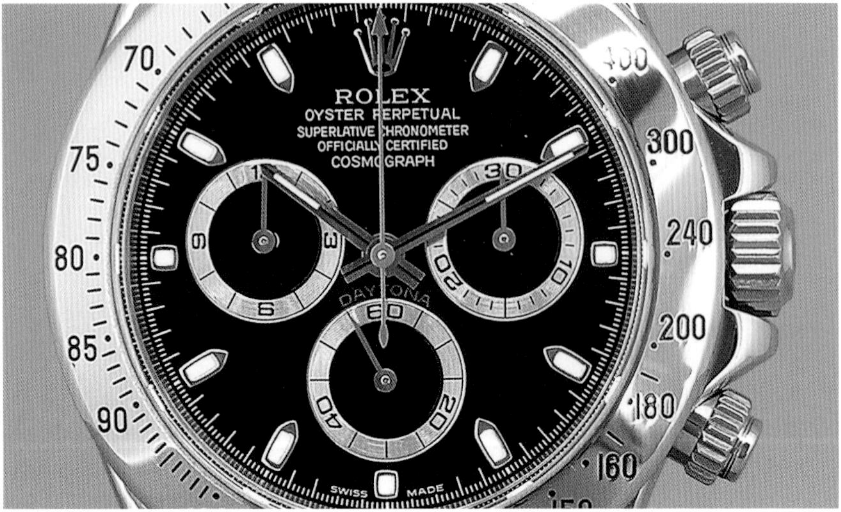

FAKE DAYTONA

The calibre inside is an imitation ETA movement (7750). For a model like this one, it's essential to actually open up the watch, since the external appearance can be very deceptive. Sometimes only the movement will reveal the difference.

ORIGINAL SUBMARINER 14060

FAKE SUBMARINER

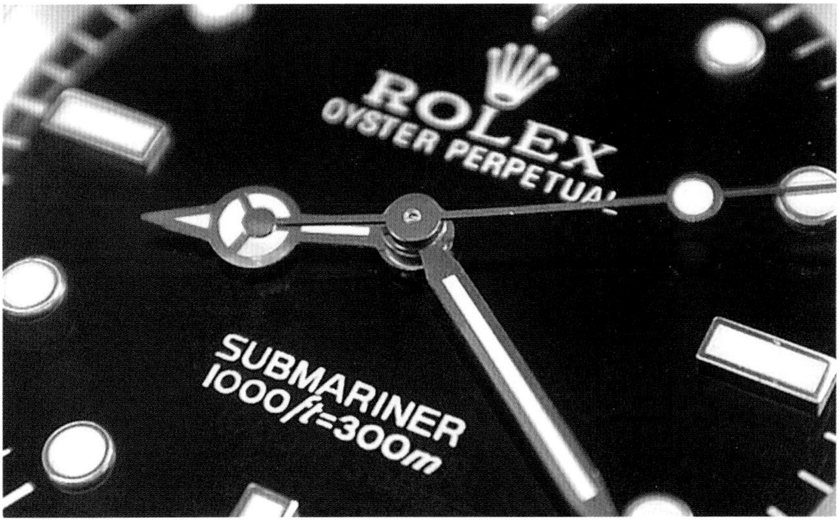

MAIN DIFFERENCES: the movement inside is an imitation ETA movement. Submariner models are the ones of which the most outwardly convincing copies are made. For a model such as this, it's essential to actually open up the watch.

ORIGINAL SUBMARINER 16610

FAKE SUBMARINER

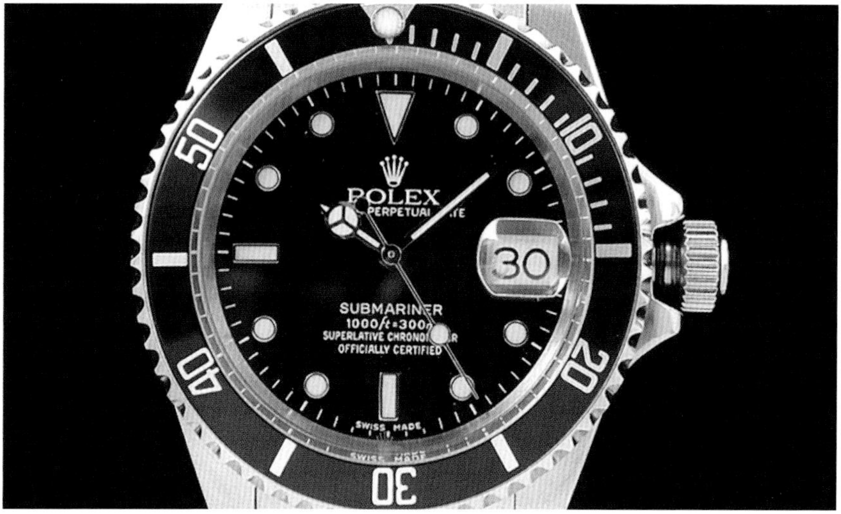

MAIN DIFFERENCES: the movement inside is an imitation ETA movement. Submariner models are the ones of which the most outwardly convincing copies are made. For a model such as this, it's essential to actually open up the watch.

ORIGINAL SUBMARINER 16610 LV

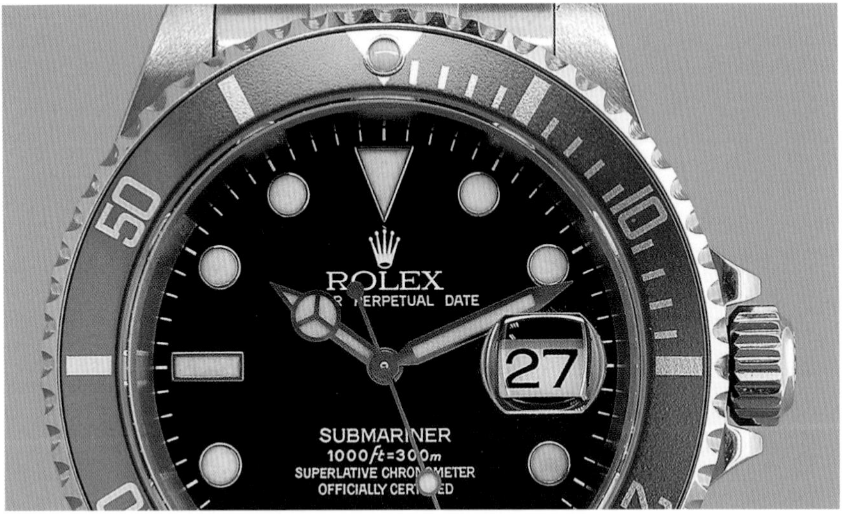

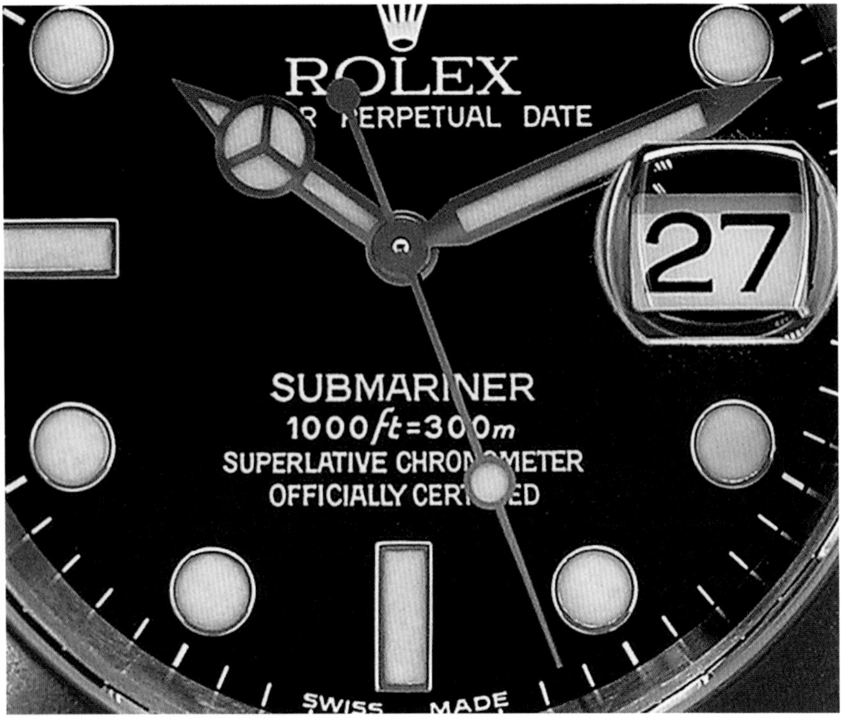

FAKE SUBMARINER

MAIN DIFFERENCES: the movement inside is an imitation ETA movement. Submariner models are the ones of which the most outwardly convincing copies are made. For a model such as this, it's essential to actually open up the watch.

ORIGINAL SUBMARINER 116619

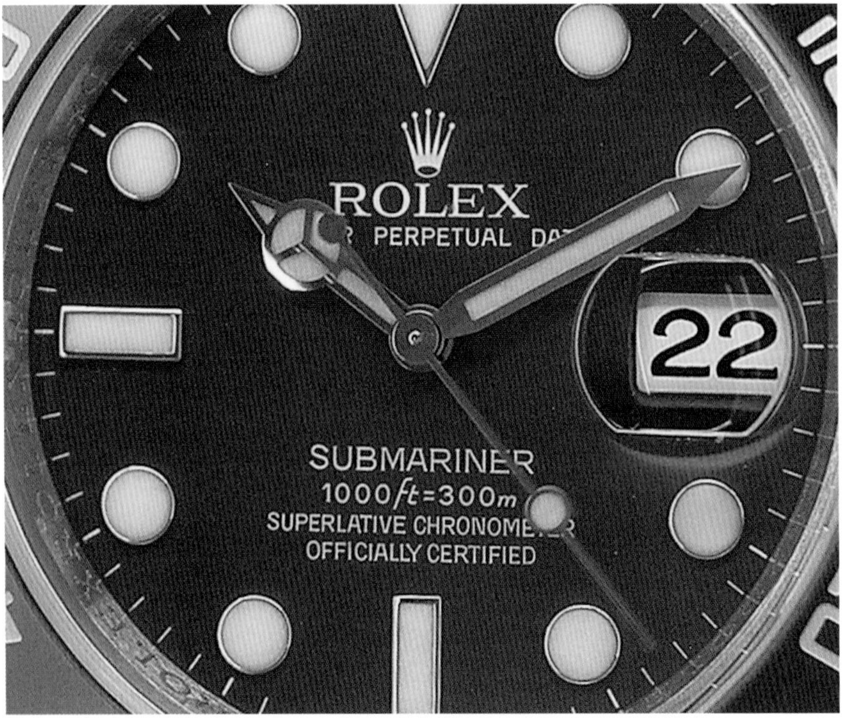

FAKE SUBMARINER

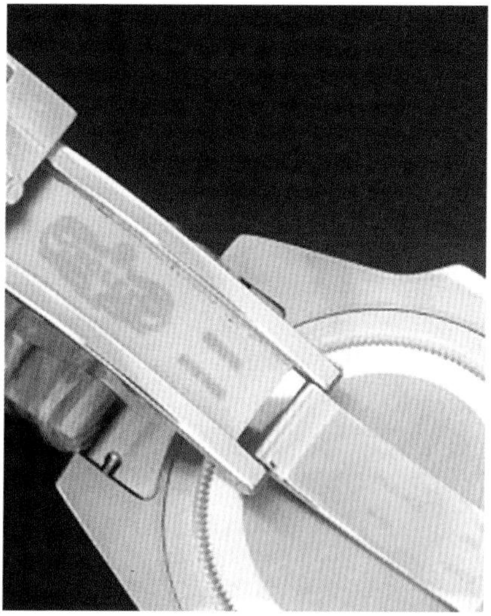

MAIN DIFFERENCES: the original is in white gold and thus very heavy. The fake is in steel, which is lighter. The movement inside is an imitation ETA movement. Submariner models are the ones of which the most outwardly convincing copies are made. By way of information, mail-order or internet purchases are best avoided for this type of model.

ORIGINAL SUBMARINER 16610 PVD

FAKE SUBMARINER

MAIN DIFFERENCES: the movement inside is an imitation ETA movement. Submariner models are the ones of which the most outwardly convincing copies are made. For a model such as this, it's essential to actually open up the watch.

ORIGINAL SUBMARINER 16613

FAKE SUBMARINER

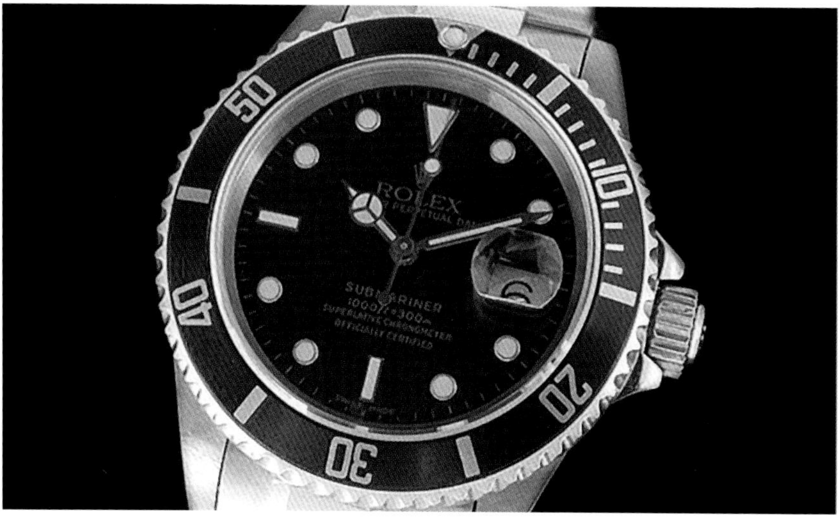

MAIN DIFFERENCES: the movement inside is an imitation ETA movement. Submariner models are the ones of which the most outwardly convincing copies are made. For a model such as this, it's essential to actually open up the watch.

ORIGINAL MILGAUSS

FAKE MILGAUSS

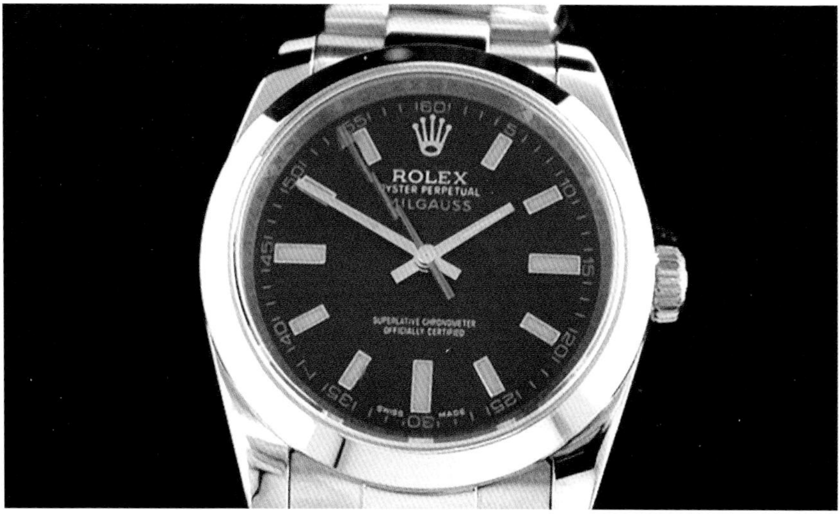

MAIN DIFFERENCES: finishing, an imitation Swiss ETA movement. Differences between the hands, meaning a shorter Luminova®-coated zone on the original (hour hand) and a longer seconds hand on the fake. Opening up the watch is strongly recommended.

ORIGINAL MILGAUSS

FAKE MILGAUSS

MAIN DIFFERENCES: finishing, an imitation Swiss ETA movement. Differences between the hands, meaning a shorter Luminova®-coated zone on the original (hour hand) and a longer seconds hand on the fake. Opening up the watch is strongly recommended.

ORIGINAL SEA-DWELLER 16600

FAKE SEA-DWELLER

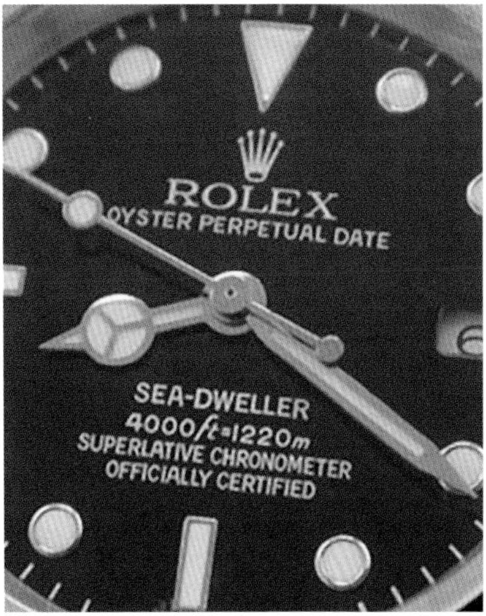

MAIN DIFFERENCES: finishing, imitation Swiss ETA movement. Small-sized winding-crown gasket on the fake (almost twice as thick on the original). For this model, it's essential to open up the watch.

ORIGINAL SEA-DWELLER DEEPSEA

FAKE SEA-DWELLER

MAIN DIFFERENCES: This is a recent watch and the differences are still very obvious (2009). Extremely thick convex glass on the original, compared with a flat glass on the fake. The thickness of the watch is also different; in most cases, the case used on fakes is the same as on the Submariner and the former Sea-Dweller models, but this is likely to change.

ORIGINAL YACHT-MASTER

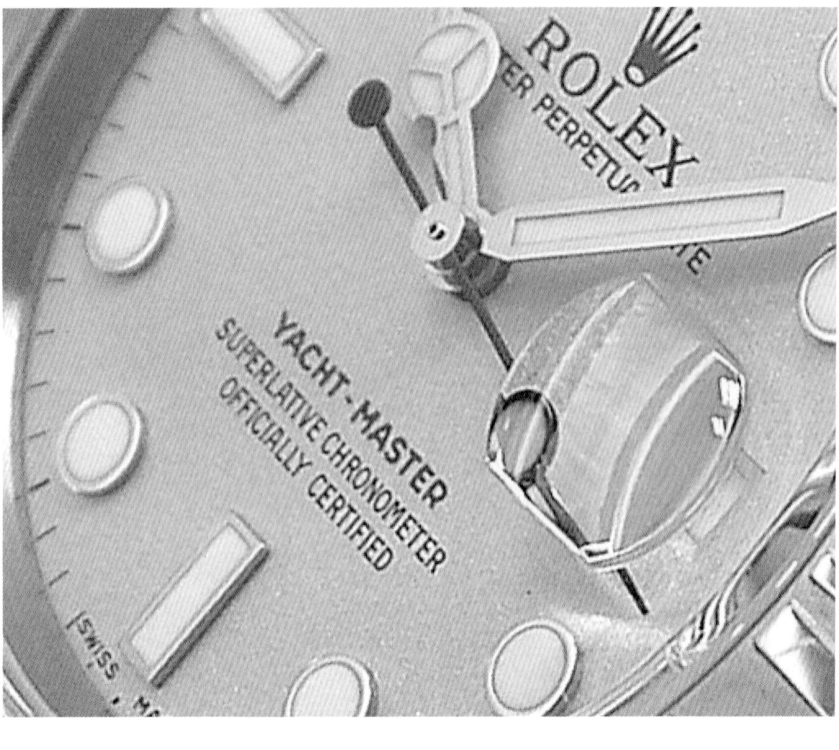

FAKE YACHT-MASTER

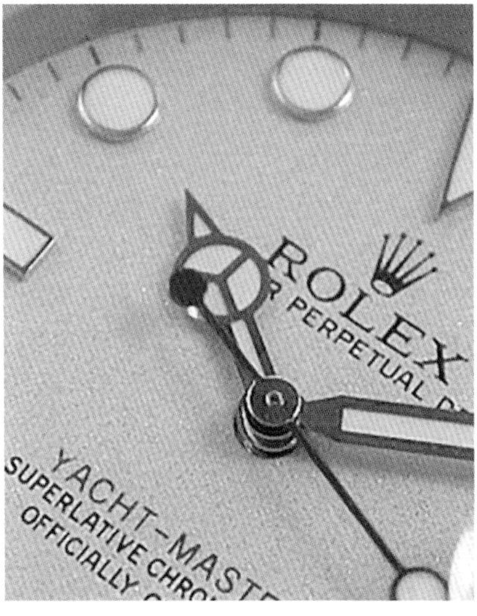

MAIN DIFFERENCES: the calibre inside is an imitation ETA movement. This model, which was still poorly copied two years ago, has now reached an impressive level of sophistication in terms of its exterior. For a model such as this, it's essential to actually open up the watch. The pictures also show the evolution of the fake movement.

ORIGINAL YACHT-MASTER II

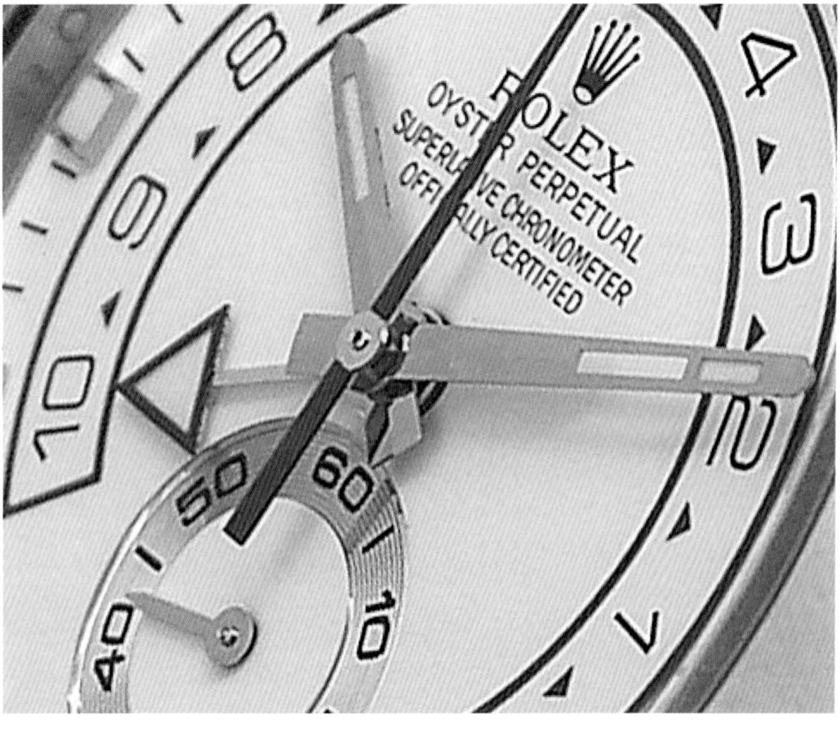

FAKE YACHT-MASTER II

MAIN DIFFERENCES: We have not seen any evolution on this model over the past two years. The fakes are poorly made and the finishing is minimal. For example, the protective lugs on the counterfeit are the same as on a Submariner, which is not at all the case on the original model.

ORIGINAL GMT-MASTER II 16710

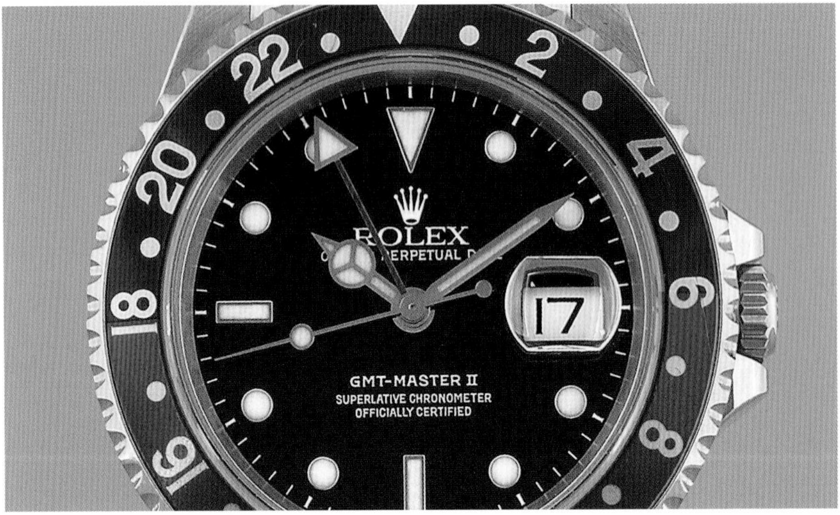

FAKE GMT-MASTER II 16710

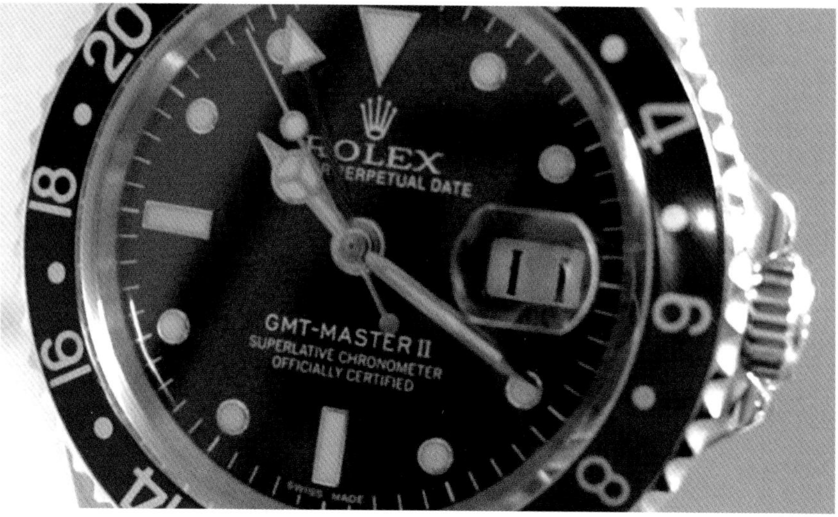

MAIN DIFFERENCES: Like the Submariner, the GMT-Master is a watch that is fairly well copied in some cases. Mail-order or internet purchases should be avoided for this type of models; it's essential to open it up in order to compare the quality of the calibre. Fakes are equipped with imitation ETA movements.

ORIGINAL GMT-MASTER II 116710

FAKE GMT-MASTER II 116710

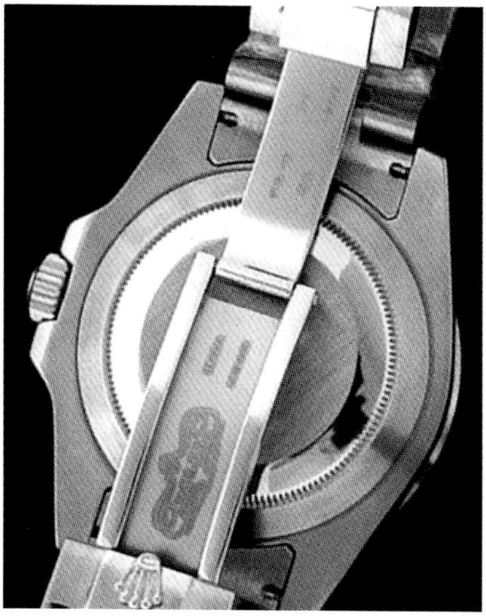

MAIN DIFFERENCES: Like the Submariner, the GMT-Master is a watch that is fairly well copied in some cases. Mail-order or internet purchases should be avoided for this type of model; it's essential to open it up in order to compare the quality of the calibre. Fakes are equipped with imitation ETA movements.

ORIGINAL GMT-MASTER II 116713

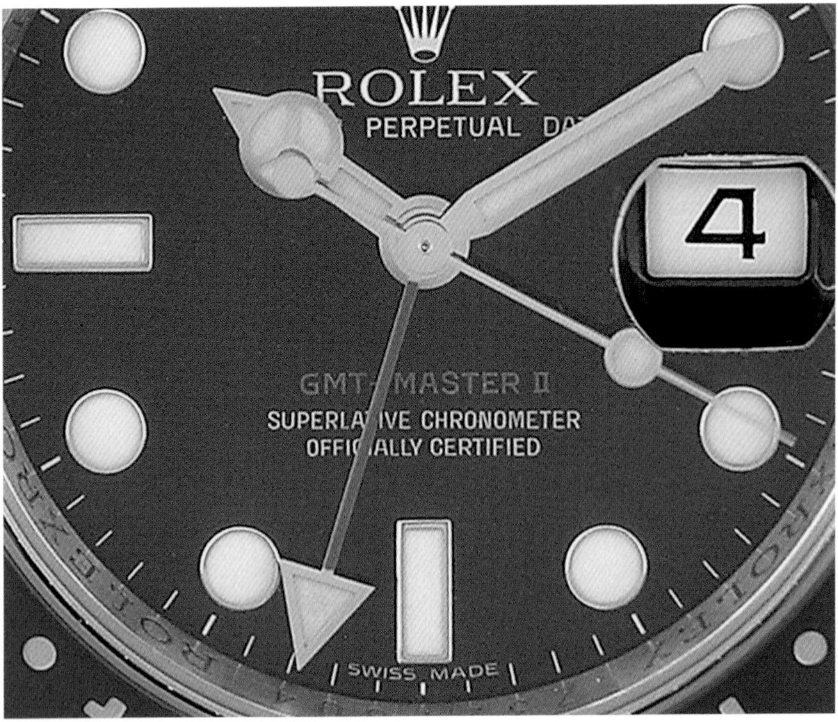

FAKE GMT-MASTER II 116713

MAIN DIFFERENCES: Like the Submariner, the GMT-Master is a watch that is fairly well copied in some cases. Mail-order or internet purchases should be avoided for this type of models; it's essential to open it up in order to compare the quality of the calibre. Fakes are equipped with imitation ETA movements.

ORIGINAL GMT-MASTER II 116718

FAKE GMT-MASTER II 116718

MAIN DIFFERENCES: the weight of the watch provides the first indication. In the case of a solid gold fake watch, and if there is still a doubt in your mind, ask for the watch to be opened so you can compare the quality of the calibre. Fakes are equipped with imitation ETA movements.

ORIGINAL EXPLORER I

FAKE EXPLORER I

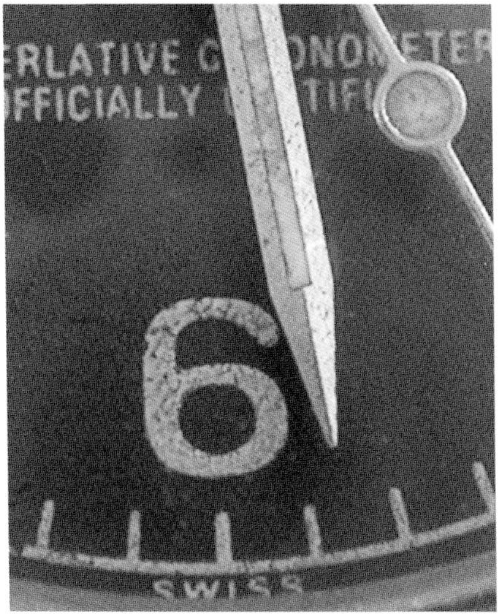

MAIN DIFFERENCES: the original is a vintage Explorer I. It's an interesting example, because the fake is also presented as a vintage and thus benefits from the wear and ageing of the various parts, which makes it harder to compare. For vintage models, we strongly recommend you consult a professional, because of the substantial risks involved.

ORIGINAL EXPLORER II

FAKE EXPLORER

MAIN DIFFERENCES: the original is a vintage Explorer II. In this case, the fake is presented as new, which is impossible since the original was produced up until the 1980s. For vintage models, we strongly recommend you consult a professional, because of the substantial risks involved.

ORIGINAL EXPLORER II 16550

FAKE EXPLORER II 16550

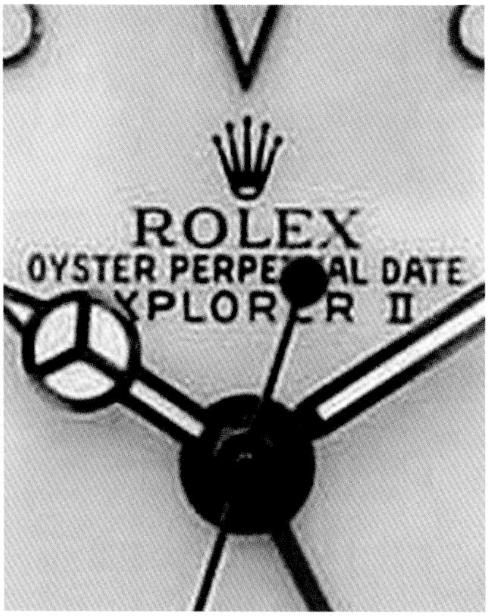

MAIN DIFFERENCES: here is a fake with an almost flawless outward appearance. Apart from the fact that the fake features circles around the indices in a different colour, an excessively large crown and the "Swiss Made" indication instead of the "Swiss T25" which appears on the original, the replica is quite impressive. For such rare models, it's better to consult a professional.

ORIGINAL TURN-O-GRAPH

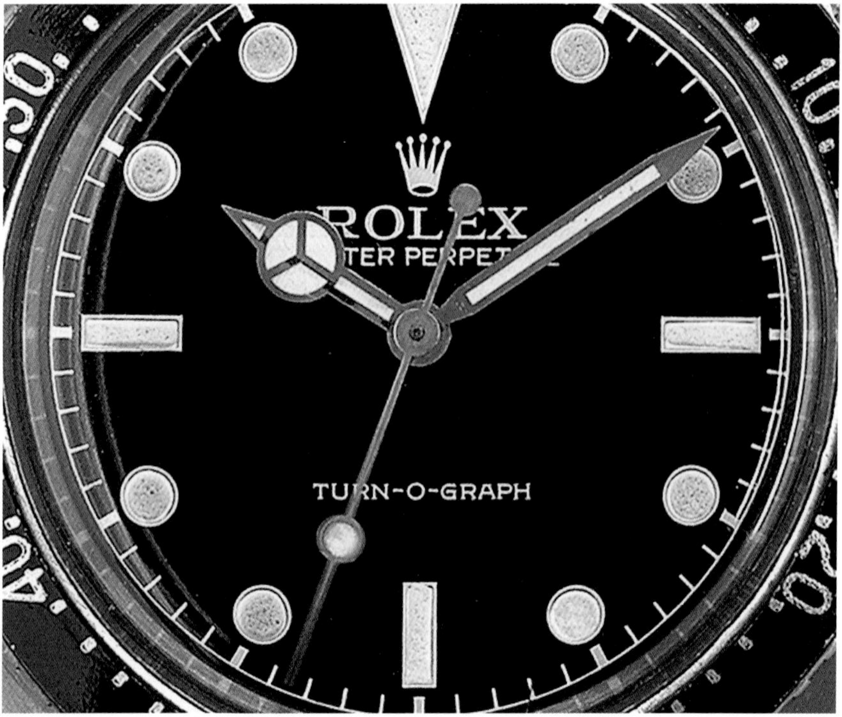

FAKE TURN-O-GRAPH

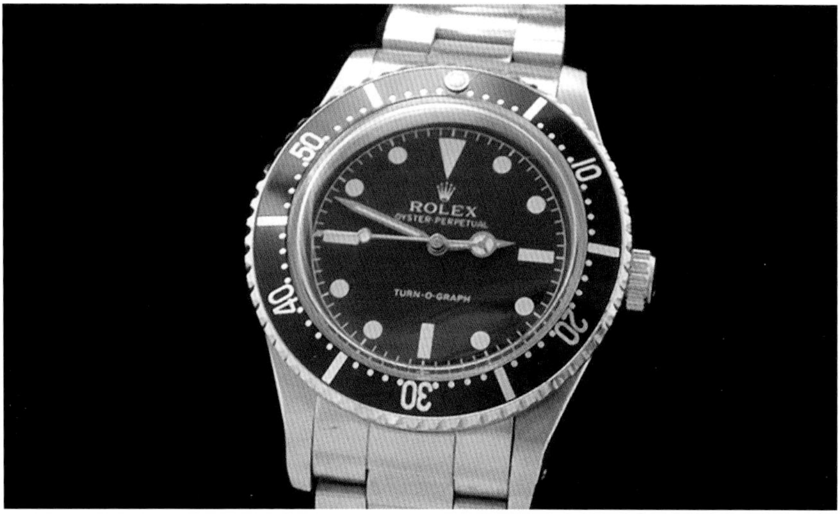

MAIN DIFFERENCES: the fake is new and comes straight from the factory. There are all kinds, which means the differences vary from one watch to another. The only noteworthy difference is the fact that the original dates back to the 1960s. But in the case of a vintage watch, you will need to consult a professional. The movement calibre will help to identify the watch.

ORIGINAL GMT-MASTER 1675

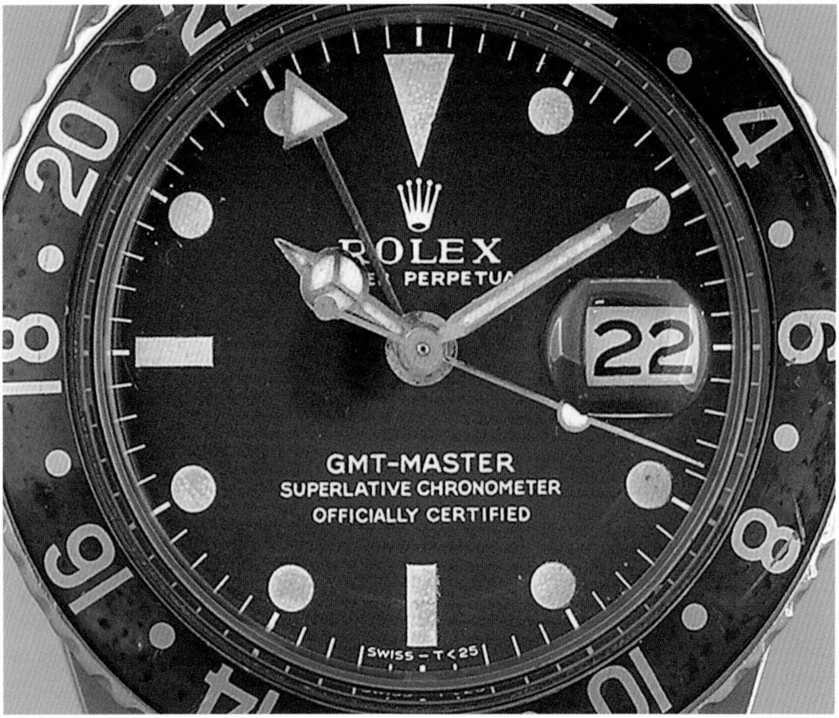

FAKE GMT-MASTER 1675

MAIN DIFFERENCES: the fake is new and comes straight from the factory. There are all kinds, which means the differences vary from one watch to another. The only noteworthy difference is the fact that the original dates back to the 1960s/70s. But in the case of a vintage watch, you will need to consult a professional. The movement calibre will help to identify the watch.

ORIGINAL GMT-MASTER 1675

FAKE GMT-MASTER 1675

MAIN DIFFERENCES: this is the same model as on the previous page, but it is worth noting certain differences. On the fake, the crown bears the three dots of the exclusive Rolex Triplock® system. This style was never used for the 1675 and the original crown bore only a single horizontal bar. The steel bezel on the fake is also that of a Submariner, and thus wider.

ORIGINAL SEA-DWELLER 1665

FAKE SEA-DWELLER 1665

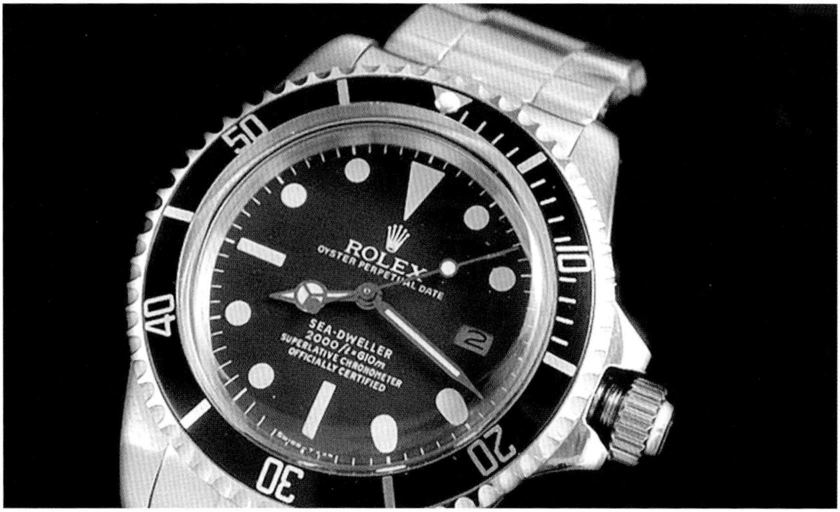

MAIN DIFFERENCES: this is also an example of a vintage watch and a brand-new fake model displaying several key differences. Machine-yellowed hour-markers on the fake, along with poor finishing that means the watch catches on clothes; bevelled hour and minute hands; and a different steel bezel. The calibre is an imitation ETA movement.

ORIGINAL SEA-DWELLER DOUBLE RED

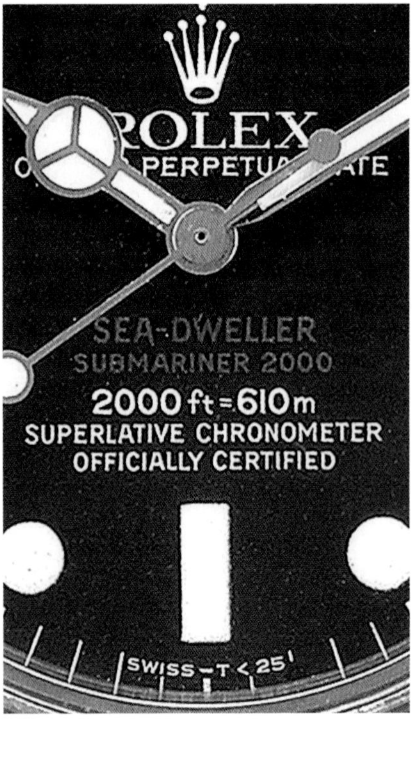

FAKE SEA-DWELLER DOUBLE RED

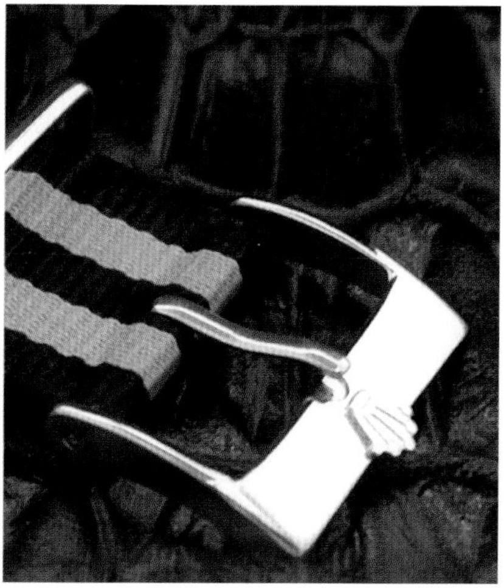

MAIN DIFFERENCES: this is also an example of a vintage watch and a brand-new fake model displaying several key differences. Machine-yellowed hour-markers on the fake, along with poor finishing that means the watch catches on clothes; bevelled hour and minute hands; and the counterfeiters have not even taken the trouble of perforating the horns that accommodate the bracelet lugs. Finally, the calibre is an imitation ETA movement.

ORIGINAL SUBMARINER 5513

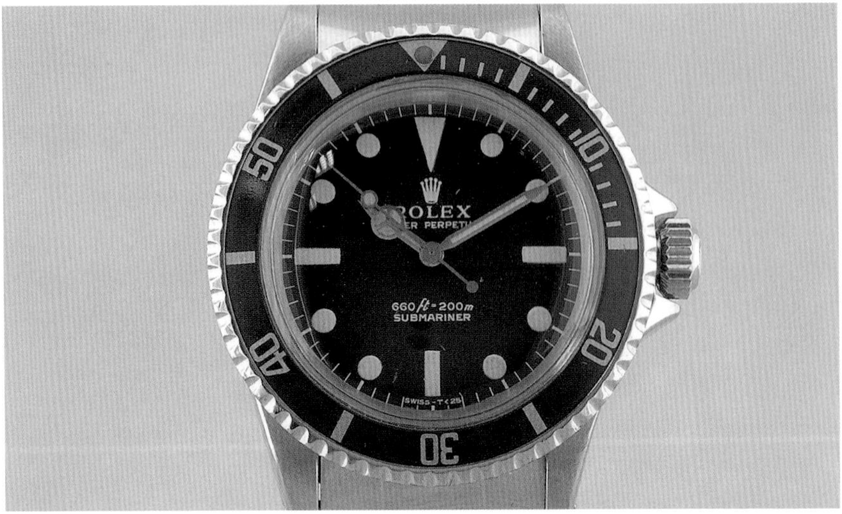

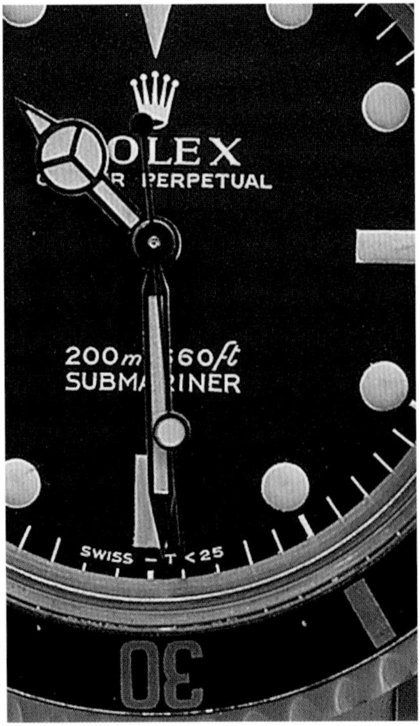

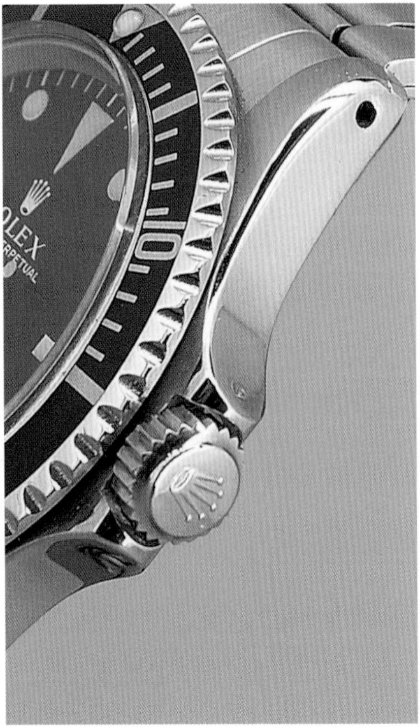

FAKE SUBMARINER 5513

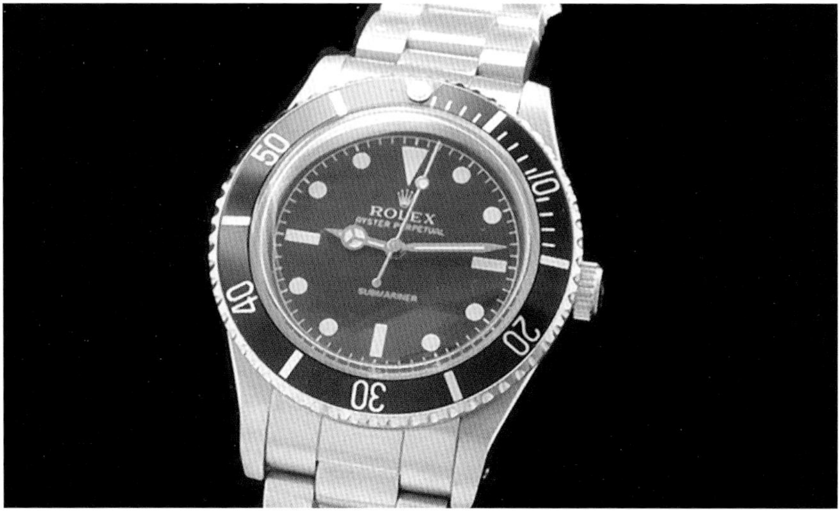

MAIN DIFFERENCES: in seeking to add "value" to the copy, the counterfeiters have made a kind of mixture by inserting details such as one of the first dials to equip the 5513 models (marked only with the word "Submariner" on its own); or a bezel with a red triangle at 12 o'clock. In this example, the watch is very old and it is impossible to find one "straight out of the workshop" like the fake presented above.

ORIGINAL SUBMARINER 5517

FAKE SUBMARINER 5517

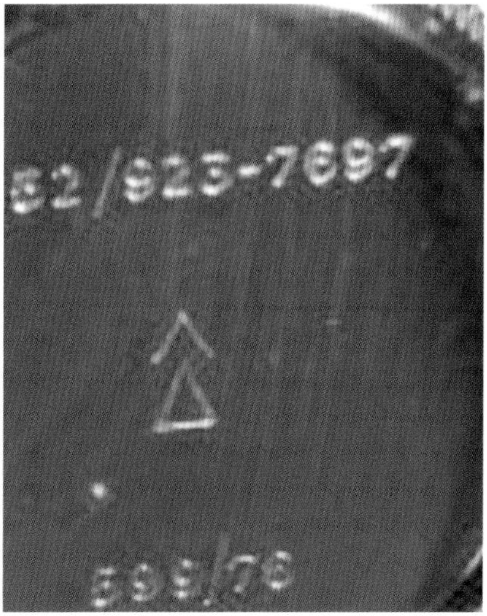

MAIN DIFFERENCES: this is a highly valued watch that will interest passionate collectors who pay attention to details. One particular detail visible here is that the original watch carries the number 5513 between the lugs and that the number 5517 appears beneath the right-hand horn. The counterfeiters have simply stamped the number 5517 on the case between the lugs.

ORIGINAL SUBMARINER 1680 RED

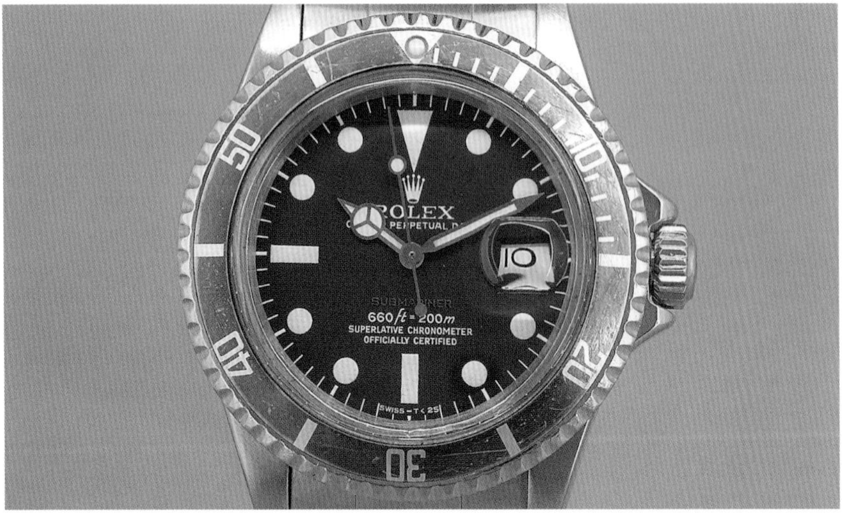

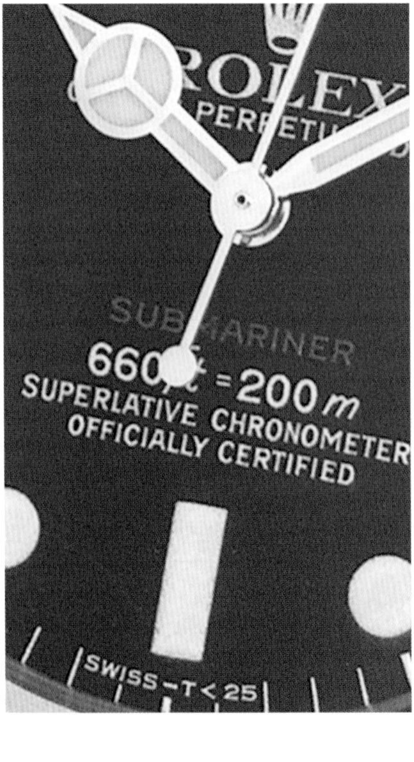

FAKE SUBMARINER 1680 RED

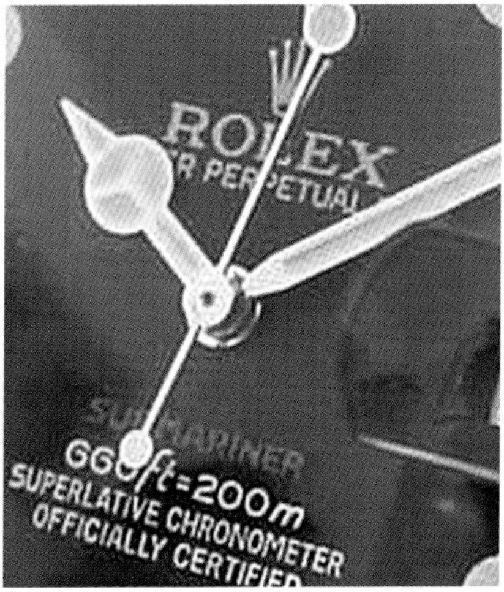

MAIN DIFFERENCES: a similar example to that of the vintage Submariner without a date display. A vintage watch and a brand-new fake model displaying several key differences. Machine-yellowed hour-markers on the fake, along with poor finishing that means the watch catches on clothes; bevelled hour and minute hands; and a different steel bezel. Finally, the calibre is an imitation ETA movement.

ORIGINAL DAYTONA 6265

FAKE DAYTONA 6265

MAIN DIFFERENCES: on most fake vintage Rolex Daytona models, the watch is equipped with an imitation automatic-winding 7750 movement, whereas the original normally houses a mechanical Valjoux 72 calibre. Another distinguishing detail is that the original measures 38 mm in diameter, and the fake 40 mm. The distance between the lugs is 18 mm for the original and 20 mm for the counterfeit, but unfortunately this may change.

ORIGINAL DAYTONA 6241 PAUL NEWMAN

FAKE DAYTONA 6241 PAUL NEWMAN

MAIN DIFFERENCES: there is major confusion among counterfeiters regarding model numbers. In this case, we have an original 6241, a model with non screw-locked pushers; and a fake marked 6263, which is a more recent model with screw-locked pushers. The fake is also equipped with an imitation automatic 7750 movement. Note that the markings on the case-back of the fake do not match the original.

ORIGINAL VINTAGE CHRONOGRAPH

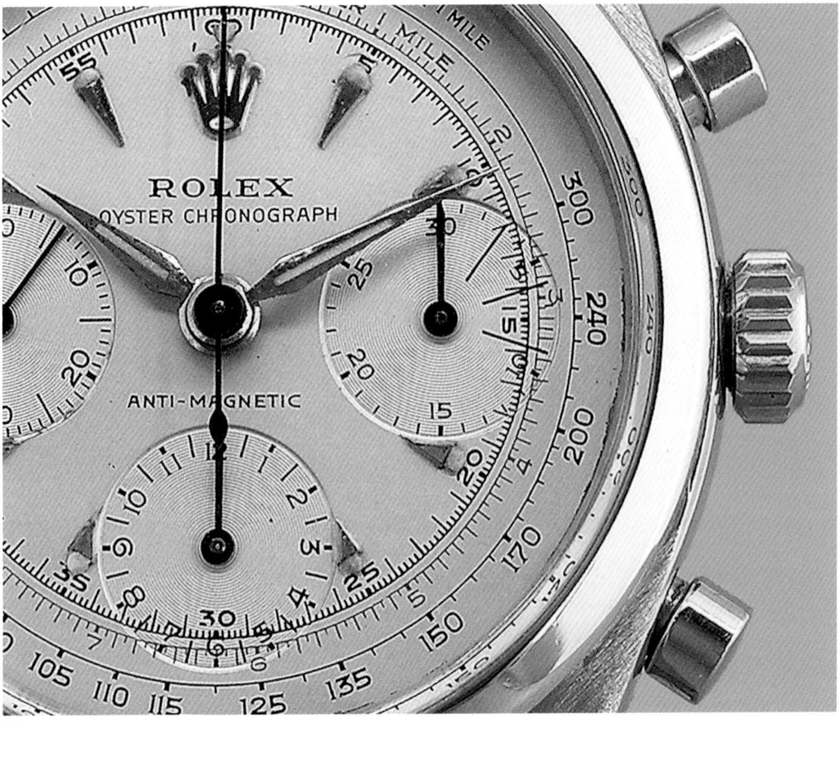

FAKE VINTAGE CHRONOGRAPH

MAIN DIFFERENCES: the counterfeiters are dealing with a 1950s watch so needless to say, the brand-new fake watch has got it all wrong. Different hour, minute and chronograph hands as well as different hour-markers, not to mention the diameter of the watch: 38mm for the original and 40mm for the fake.

ORIGINAL ROLEX MOVEMENTS

ORIGINAL ROLEX MOVEMENTS

MAIN CHARACTERISTICS: here are some original movements that will help you to appreciate the quality of the finishing applied by the brand. The movement pictured at the top is a 1950s movement (GMT-Master 6542); note the superior quality of the markings for the period.

FAKE ROLEX MOVEMENTS

FAKE ROLEX MOVEMENTS

MAIN DIFFERENCES: even though considerable efforts have been made in terms of imitation, the calibres are far from comparable. Above, an imitation Lemania movement used in some fake vintage Daytona models. This copy does not enable the watch to handle the small chronograph hour function separately. The latter is therefore not functional.

ORIGINAL ROYAL OAK OFFSHORE

FAKE ROYAL OAK OFFSHORE

MAIN DIFFERENCES: significant progress has been made in the area of counterfeits over the past two years. Today, most brands are affected. On the model pictured opposite, the two noteworthy differences are the difference in weight, the imitation crocodile leather strap on the fake and the difference in the font used for the date (see the number 2). Like fake Rolex watches, the fake Audemars Piguet is equipped with an imitation ETA movement.

ORIGINAL ROYAL OAK OFFSHORE

FAKE ROYAL OAK OFFSHORE

MAIN DIFFERENCES: the quality of finishing is a significant point to look out for on fakes. The main brands go to great lengths to achieve a very high standard of finish, which is the key focus for the majority of them. The quality of the brushed surface of the steel shown here, as well as the quality of the circular satin-brushing (which is coarser on the fakes) are the kind of details that will help identify the watch.

ORIGINAL ROYAL OAK KASPAROV

FAKE ROYAL OAK KASPAROV

MAIN DIFFERENCES: the model presented here has the advantage of being fitted with a transparent back (sapphire crystal case-back). Look no further, since the fake movement immediately shows that this is a poor imitation.

ORIGINAL BELL & ROSS BR 01-92

FAKE BELL & ROSS BR 01-92

MAIN DIFFERENCES: for a company producing fairly straightforward watches, such as this BR 01-92, identification is a trickier issue. In a case such as this, we strongly advise against making any mail-order or internet purchases, since photos provide no chance of spotting a fake – especially if the movement is not visible.

ORIGINAL BELL & ROSS BR 01-94

FAKE BELL & ROSS BR 01-94

MAIN DIFFERENCES: apart from the date aperture, which has a circle around it on the fake model, few details offer a chance of checking that the watch is genuine. Opening it, which is indispensable, reveals a fake yellow movement, as is the case with the majority of fakes. But here too, this point can be changed. Also note the poor-quality finishing of the pushers on the fake model.

ORIGINAL BELL & ROSS BR 01-97

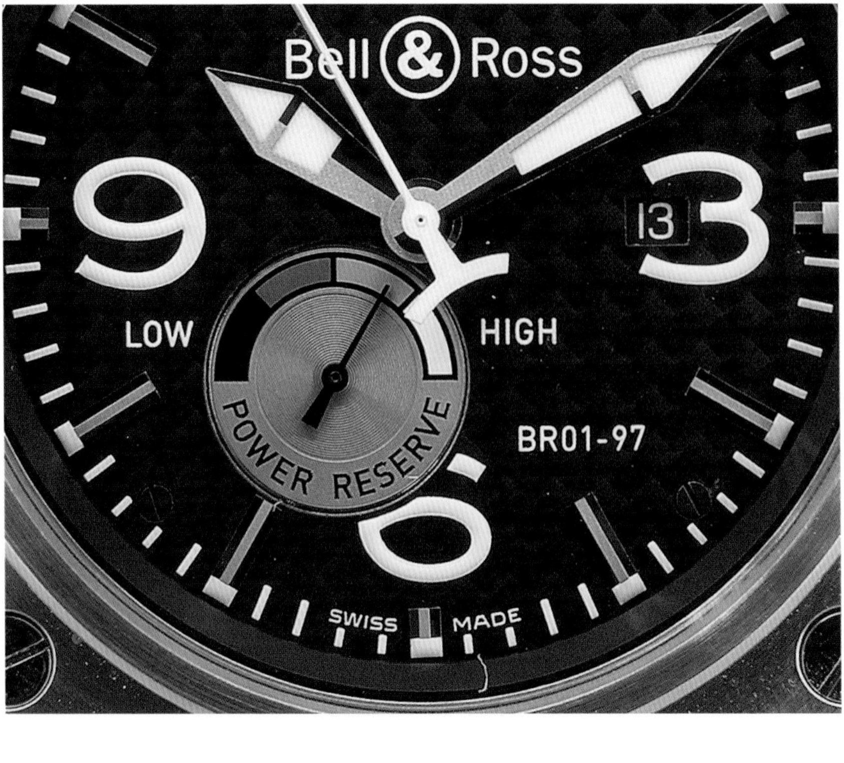

FAKE BELL & ROSS BR 01-97

MAIN DIFFERENCES: for a gold watch such as this, the difference in weight provides a fast means of identification. Note the large chronograph seconds hand, which is made of simple metal on the fake and painted white on the original.

ORIGINAL BREGUET TYPE XX

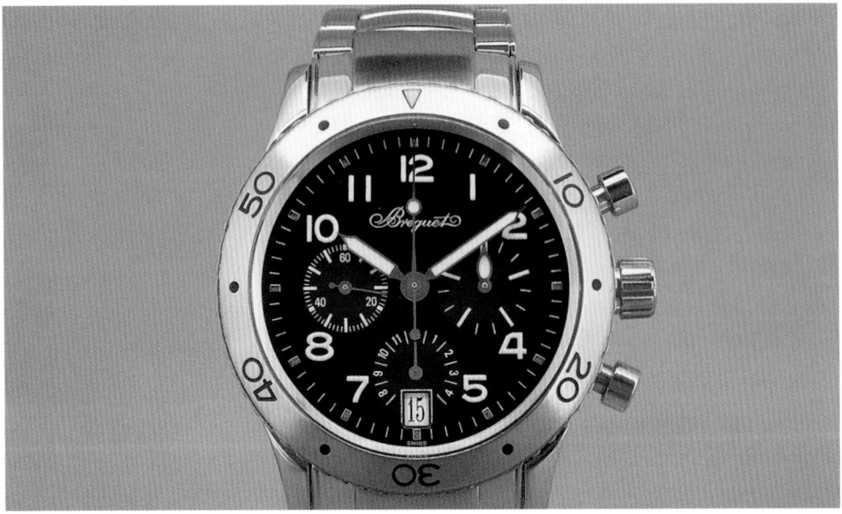

FAKE BREGUET TYPE XX

MAIN DIFFERENCES: there is no real problem with identifying this model. The fake movement fitted by the counterfeiters is a far cry from the brand's characteristic high-quality finish. Also note the font difference on the date display. The finishes, which are not visible on the photos, clearly reveal that this is not a real Breguet watch.

ORIGINAL BREGUET TYPE XX

FAKE BREGUET TYPE XX

MAIN DIFFERENCES: the same all-gold model. The significant weight difference is enough to tell them apart. The quality of the finishing also facilitates fast identification of the fake: the date display font, the quality of the markings, the cheap gold plating, the font used for the chronograph numerals, etc.

ORIGINAL BREITLING AVENGER

FAKE BREITLING AVENGER

MAIN DIFFERENCES: counterfeiters have lavished considerable effort on certain brands, particularly the most sought-after. Nonetheless, the quality of finishing is distinctly inferior and, in addition to the date display font and hour numerals, touching a fake watch gives a distinct impression of poor quality.

ORIGINAL BREITLING AVENGER SEAWOLF

FAKE BREITLING AVENGER SEAWOLF

ORIGINAL BREITLING CHRONOMAT

FAKE BREITLING CHRONOMAT

MAIN DIFFERENCES: the best way of distinguishing a fake watch from a real one as far as this model is concerned is to open the case and check the quality of the movement. In this case, such a test reveals a poor-quality imitation ETA calibre, which can be rapidly identified as soon as the watch is opened.

ORIGINAL BREITLING NAVITIMER MONTBRILLANT DATORA

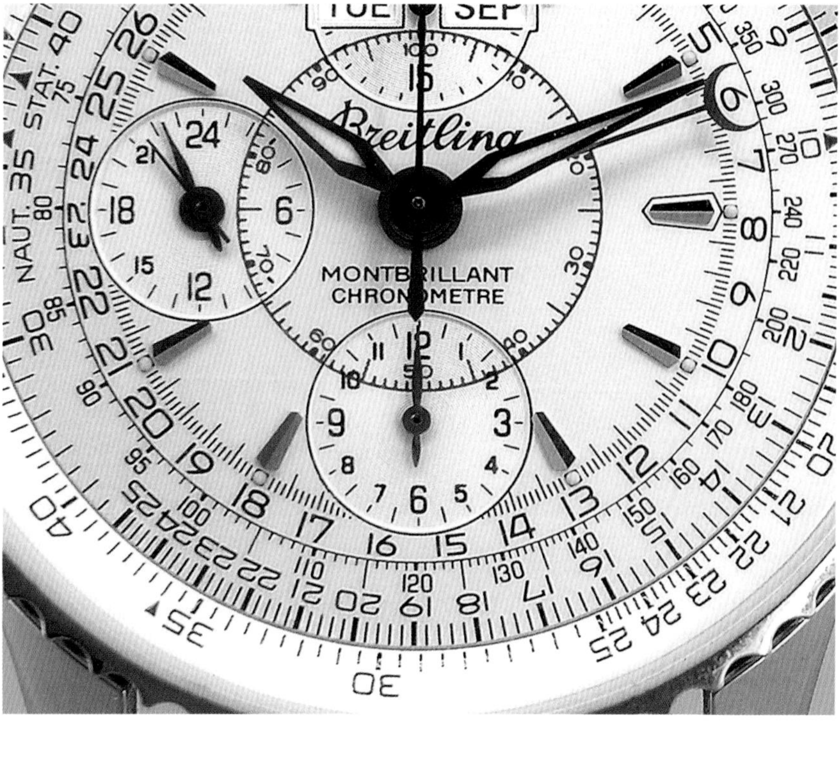

FAKE BREITLING NAVITIMER MONTBRILLANT DATORA

MAIN DIFFERENCES: the counterfeiters have made an effort as far as the movement of this watch is concerned. But it's still not up to Swiss quality. Moreover, the painting on the dial is inferior and the red counter circles look more like the result of an inferior stamping operation than a genuine aesthetic feature.

ORIGINAL BREITLING FOR BENTLEY

FAKE BREITLING FOR BENTLEY

MAIN DIFFERENCES: here's a typical example of a poorly finished counterfeit. The treatment of the steel on the case-back has been neglected: poor brushing, poor-quality screw caps, etc. The photo speaks for itself. The weight of the watch (thanks to the high-quality steel Breitling used for the real watch) along with the movement are the best assets for identification.

ORIGINAL PASHA

FAKE PASHA

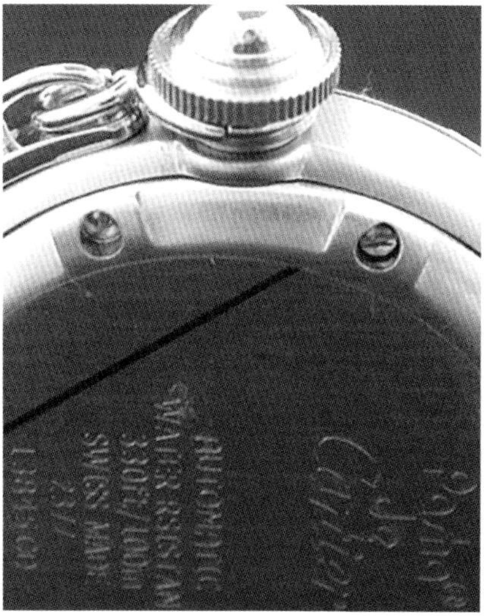

MAIN DIFFERENCES: this is an all-gold model, which means the weight will be the first sign of a fake. Note the difference between the hands as well as the absence of a sapphire cabochon on the winding-crown of the fake.

ORIGINAL PASHA POWER RESERVE

FAKE PASHA POWER RESERVE

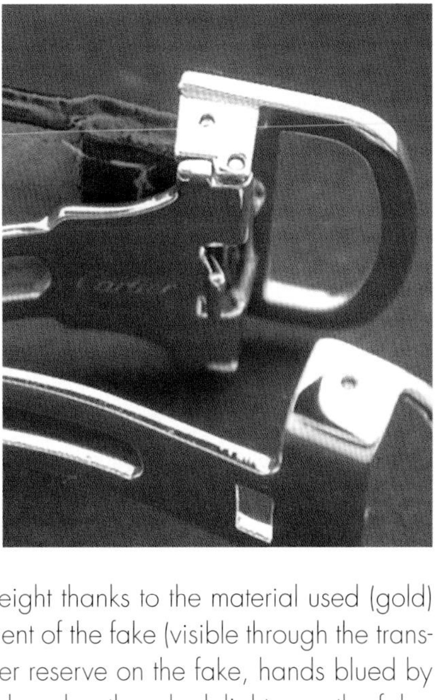

MAIN DIFFERENCES: a difference in weight thanks to the material used (gold) used for the original, poor-quality movement of the fake (visible through the transparent case-back), the back-to-front power reserve on the fake, hands blued by anodization instead of flame-blued, which makes them look lighter on the fake. However, the weight is the best means of identification.

ORIGINAL STEEL SANTOS 100

FAKE STEEL SANTOS 100

MAIN DIFFERENCES: this is a watch that absolutely must be opened. The rare details appearing on the outside enable counterfeiters to copy it quite easily. Few people are able to compare two steels of different quality. However, the movement serves to identify the watch: a poor-quality ETA imitation held inside the case by a pitiful piece of plastic.

ORIGINAL SANTOS 100 CHRONO

FAKE SANTOS 100 CHRONO

MAIN DIFFERENCES: here is the same chronograph model, which also needs to be opened. The movement serves to identify the watch: a poor-quality 7750 fake held inside the case by a pitiful piece of plastic. The quality of the steel is inferior on the entire watch, if you happen to be capable of comparing two different steels.

ORIGINAL SANTOS ROADSTER

FAKE SANTOS ROADSTER

MAIN DIFFERENCES: while not easy to spot on the photos, the poor quality of the finishing is visible at first glance. But it's still necessary to open the watch. Inside is a fake Swiss movement in yellow metal.
The hands on the fake model are anodized rather than heat-treated.

ORIGINAL J12 CERAMIC AND STEEL

FAKE J12 CERAMIC GOLD/STEEL

MAIN DIFFERENCES: for this best-selling model, the counterfeiters have made a genuine effort and have made a so-called "good quality" copy. It is good quality that is only skin deep, however, because while they have been at pains to replicate the watch's winding rotor, the movement behind it does not match up and is of poor quality (it is visible through the transparent case-back).

ORIGINAL J12 CHRONOGRAPH

FAKE J12 CHRONOGRAPH

MAIN DIFFERENCES: this is a watch that absolutely must be opened, since even though the finishes are rather different in some respects, it's not easy to identify the watch at first glance. Opening it up will reveal a poor imitation of the 7750 chronograph movement.

ORIGINAL J12 SUPERLEGGERA

FAKE J12 SUPERLEGGERA

MAIN DIFFERENCES: different finishing, particularly in terms of the quality of the dial and the "Superleggera" marking, which is coarser on the fake. Apart from that, it is advisable to open the watch. On the watch pictured above, you will note a major error in the marking of the chronograph measurements, but this may vary from one fake to another.

ORIGINAL MILLE MIGLIA GRAN TURISMO

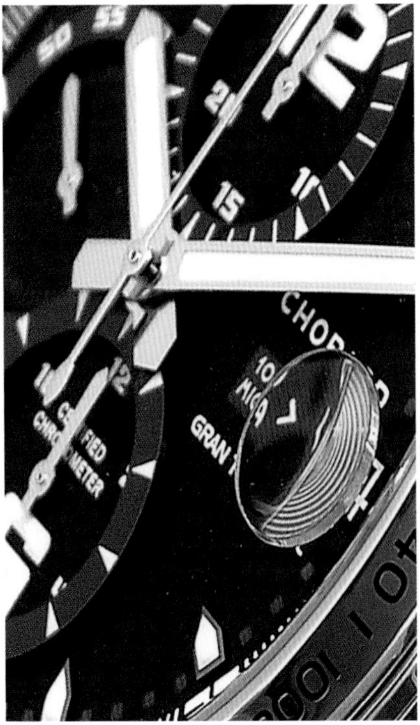

FAKE MILLE MIGLIA GRAND TURISMO

MAIN DIFFERENCES: this is a fairly good copy from the outside. The finishing is well done and even some of the materials used are similar to the original (e.g. titanium). Here too, it is important to take time to examine the movement. The finishing of the markings and the various engravings are somewhat inferior on the fake, as are the movement components.

ORIGINAL LA STRADA

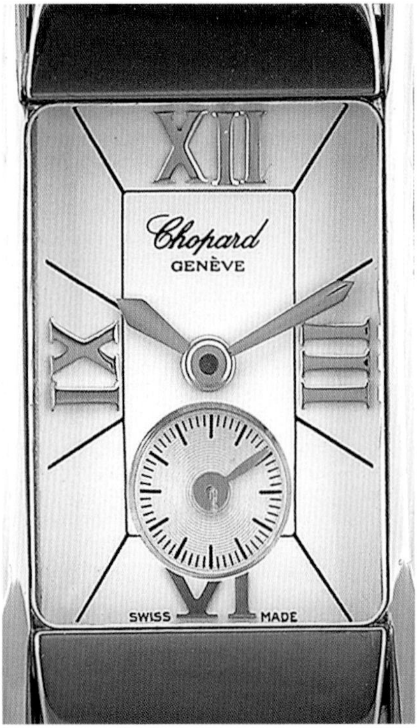

FAKE LA STRADA

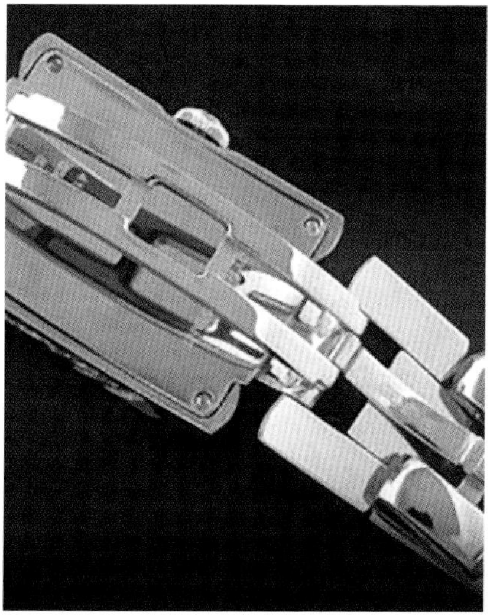

MAIN DIFFERENCES: this type of model also attracts counterfeiters. If you are a jewellery connoisseur, you can already detect the poor quality of the "stones" used on the fake. The weight is also different, since the fake watch is in steel and not in white gold like the original.

ORIGINAL CASABLANCA STEEL DATE

FAKE CASABALANCA STEEL DATE

MAIN DIFFERENCES: the Franck Muller brand, known for the quality of its materials and for the variety of its models, has undoubtedly managed to confuse counterfeiters regarding the choice of hands, the position of date displays and other details. Open the watch and the movement will erase any potential remaining doubts.

ORIGINAL CASABLANCA CHRONOGRAPH

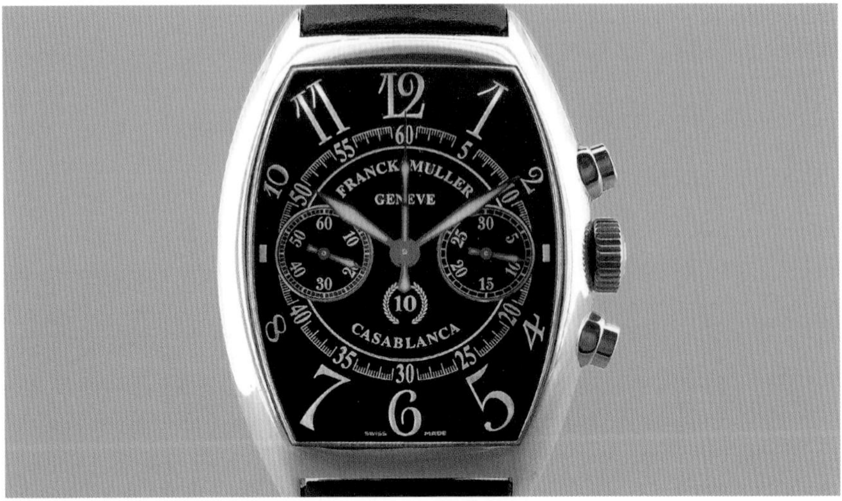

FAKE CASABLANCA CHRONOGRAPH

ORIGINAL COLOR DREAMS

FAKE COLOR DREAMS

MAIN DIFFERENCES: in addition to the noteworthy difference in product quality, there are also a number of external differences such as the font, the anodized hands (rather than flame-blued as on the original), as well as the axis of the minute/hour hand. The calibre inside the fake is as usual a poor-quality fake ETA movement.

ORIGINAL CHRONOFIGHTER OVERSIZE

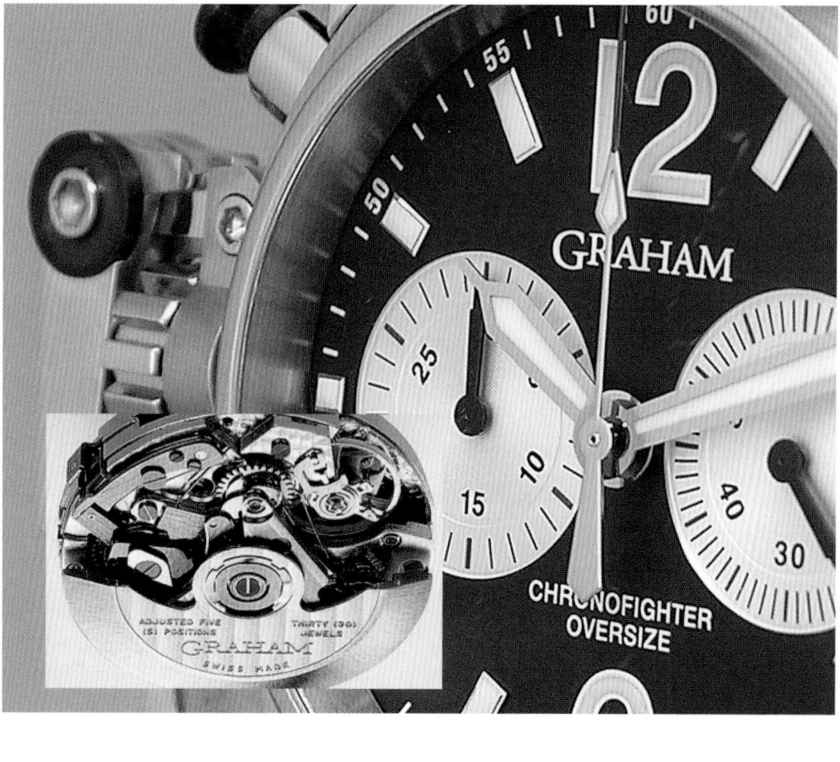

FAKE CHRONFIGHTER OVERSIZE

MAIN DIFFERENCES: although they are not clearly visible on the photos, the main differences between the real and fake watches lie in the finishes. The winding crown, for example, is rather rough on the fake compared with the original. Nonetheless, even when open, this watch is fairly hard to identify for anyone not accustomed to such an exercise.

ORIGINAL CARBON/GOLD BIG BANG

Hublot is a brand that has come under strong attack from counterfeiters over the past two years. The brand produces high-quality watches that are extremely well finished, which is not the case for the fakes. But this is not visible on the photos. Any identification must involve actually touching the watch in question in order to check the weight of the gold models and all the other details. The counterfeits will always show unsatisfactory finishing in certain areas, a flaw that does not exist with genuine watches by Hublot, which is concerned with providing customers with perfectly crafted high-end watches to match the brand image. The calibres have been copied and now feature a number of details that are almost identical to the original watches.
In 2009, Hublot, driven by a concern to fight the scourge of counterfeits, launched an extremely effective electronic identity card.

Unfortunately, many people who buy previously owned watches are more interested in getting a "good deal" than obtaining the original documents when making a transaction. But Hublot's CEO Jean-Claude Biver has not developed this system on a whim and was quick to grasp the fact that the brand needed to develop substantial means of fighting the fakers. This approach is a genuine counter-attack that deserves to be praised in this book. But what about watches that were purchased before this system was put in place? Hublot has duly considered this issue and everyone who acquired a Hublot watch before 2009 has the possibility of sending it back to the manufacturer so that it may be given the same treatment as newly produced watches, and then returned to its owner along with its identity card.

The following pages show photos of the various fairly impressive fake models that will help you see why the initiative taken by CEO Mr Jean-Claude Biver is a giant leap forward in this field.

It is thus vital to demand the original papers and the electronic card when making a purchase... unless you happen to be a qualified expert.

ORIGINAL BIG BANG ALL BLACK (250-PIECE LIMITED EDITION)

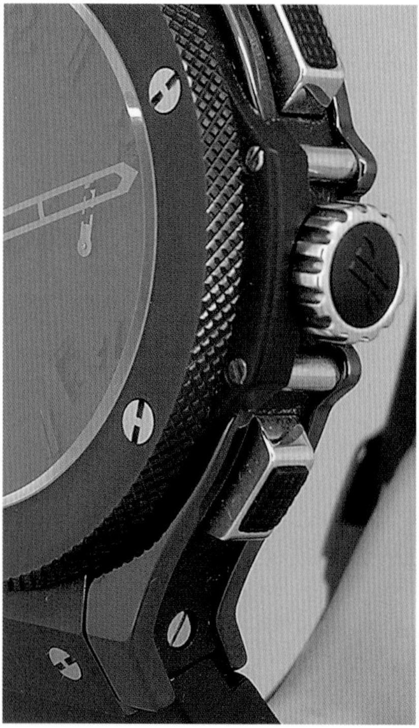

FAKE BIG BANG ALL BLACK

ORIGINAL BIG BANG CERAMIC

FAKE BIG BANG CERAMIC

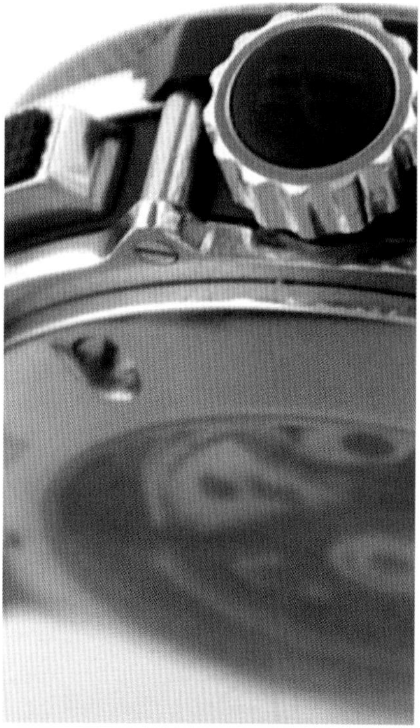

ORIGINAL BIG BANG GOLD AND DIAMONDS

FAKE BIG BANG GOLD AND DIAMONDS

ORIGINAL BIG BANG AYRTON SENNA

FAKE BIG BANG AYRTON SENNA

ORIGINAL BIG BANG CAPPUCCINO 250-PIECE LIMITED EDITION

FAKE BIG BANG RED LIMITED EDITION

ORIGINAL BIG BANG COURCHEVEL YACHT CLUB 250-PIECE LIMITED EDITION

FAKE BIG BANG MONACO YACHT CLUB LIMITED EDITION

ORIGINAL TRIPLE DATE MOON-PHASE CHRONOGRAPH

FAKE TRIPLE DATE MOON-PHASE CHRONOGRAPH

MAIN DIFFERENCES: at first glance, one might be tempted to say that these two watches show very few differences and that the fake is quite impressive. But that's not really so. The brand is not greatly affected by this particular counterfeit in that the manufacturers have made an extremely poor-quality fake. But as with all the others, you'll need to actually have it in your hand in order to realize that.

ORIGINAL SEAMASTER 007

FAKE SEAMASTER 007

Like the other prestigious brands, Omega is no exception to the curse of being subject to counterfeits. Once again, however, the fakes are more impressive in terms of their appearance than for the quality of their production. Each model reveals noteworthy differences such as are shown above: the tail-ends of the spiral motif symbolizing the barrel of the famous James Bond pistol are superimposed on the indices on the fake, whereas on the original there are no indices in this positions.

ORIGINAL SEAMASTER 007 CASINO ROYALE

FAKE SEAMASTER 007 CASINO ROYALE

Even though some fakes may seem well made at first glance, you will ALWAYS find differences and a lack of the hard-earned expertise possessed by the great Swiss brands. Such is definitely the case with this Seamaster, which has a poorly made case-back and an imitation ETA movement.

ORIGINAL SPEEDMASTER SPECIAL EDITIONS

MISSION TO MARS

SNOOPY

ORIGINAL SPEEDMASTER SPECIAL EDITIONS

SPACE WALK

WORN ON THE MOON

FAKE SPEEDMASTER SPECIAL EDITIONS

FAKE SPEEDMASTER SPECIAL EDITIONS

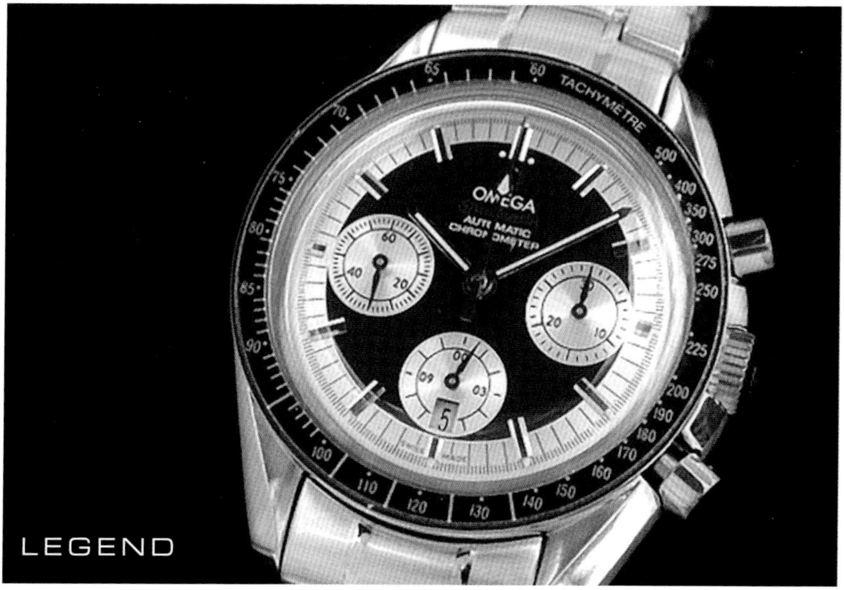

LEGEND

50th ANNIVERSARY

ORIGINAL LUMINOR MARINA

FAKE LUMINOR MARINA

Panerai has only recently begun to use proprietary movements in its watches. This is an excellent means of highlighting the fine workmanship of its products, of taking its place among the major watch brands, as well as an effective way of dealing with the counterfeit issue. By setting the standard very high in terms of quality, I believe the brand has put an end for a certain period of time to the problem of fakes bearing its name. In the following pages, we will therefore look at the models not equipped with movements that the brand has invented, developed, built and assembled in-house.

ORIGINAL LUMINOR 1950

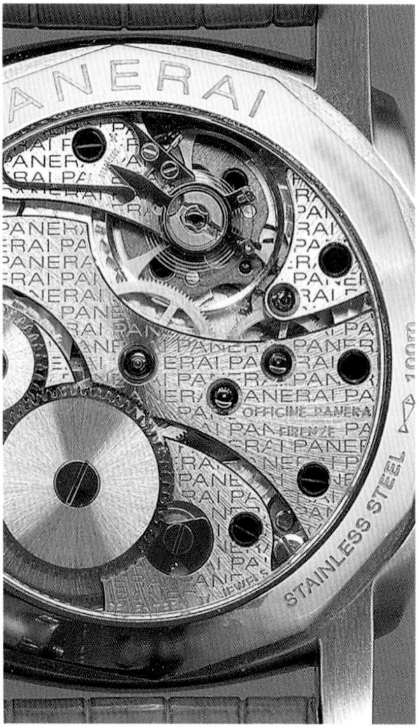

FAKE LUMINOR 1950

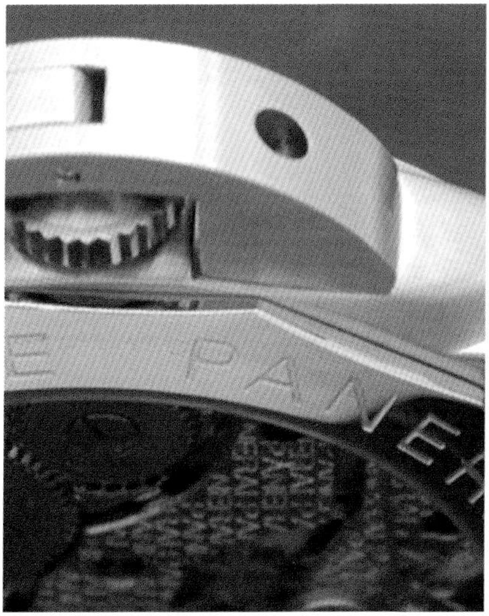

While Panerai was busy developing its new movements, the counterfeiters were doing their utmost to improve the "visual quality" of their "products". But even though this Luminor 1950, including the movement, closely resembles the original, the weight and the finishing (which can only be seen first hand and unfortunately not on a photo) nonetheless serve to tell them apart.

ORIGINAL LUMINOR DAYLIGHT

FAKE LUMINOR DAYLIGHT

Compared with the kind of fakes one used to find two years or more ago, the quality has been improved. I am prepared to speak of quality here, because it is truly the case. The fake movement is also a detailed and faithful copy. It is not of course the original movement, but an imitation 7750 calibre that will doubtless keep the fake watch running properly for several years. For this model, it's essential to open it up to view the movement.

ORIGINAL LUMINOR GMT NORTH POLE

FAKE LUMINOR GMT ARKTOS

Here's another model that will need to be opened. Models with solid backs are often equipped with yellow gold imitation ETA movements in order to save money. Unfortunately for devotees of "understated" no-frills watches, copies of such models are fairly easy to achieve, since today's fakers have cutting-edge equipment.

ORIGINAL LUMINOR LOGO

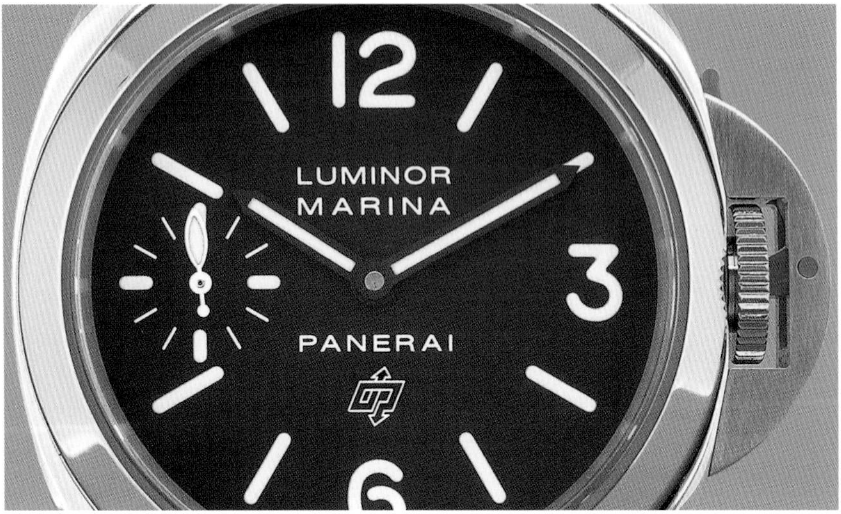

FAKE LUMINOR LOGO

This model is virtually impossible to identify without opening up the case. Sad to say, even when dealing with a non-authorized "professional", I recommend that you ask them to open up the watch, especially for this type of timepiece.

ORIGINAL LUMINOR POWER RESERVE

FAKE LUMINOR POWER RESERVE

ORIGINAL LUMINOR SUBMERSIBLE

FAKE LUMINOR SUBMERSIBLE

ORIGINAL RADIOMIR BLACK SEAL

FAKE RADIOMIR BLACK SEAL

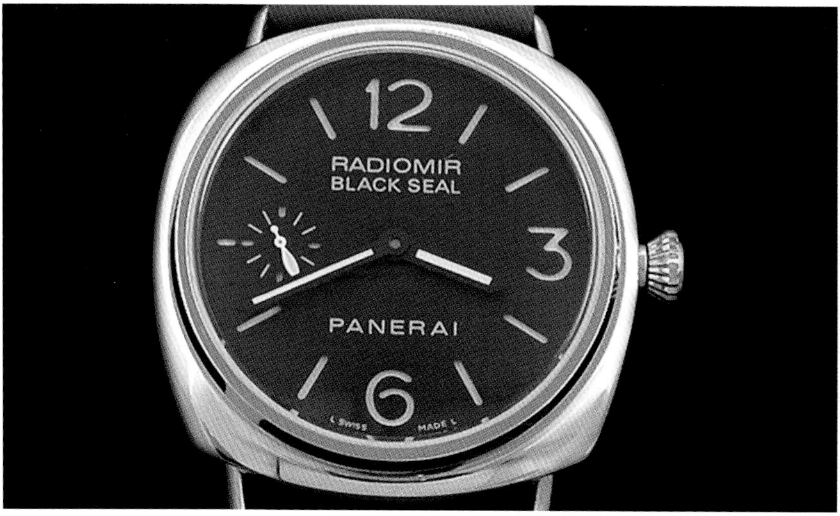

ORIGINAL RADIOMIR PAM 163

FAKE RADIOMIR PAM 163

Fortunately, there are still some models that are identifiable at a glance, such as this limited series by the brand. This model has remained unchanged since it started to be copied. Collectors need not worry, because the date has still not been added on the fake and the calibre is still a poor-quality imitation Lemania movement.

ORIGINAL AQUATIMER

FAKE AQUATIMER

This is another brand that has been severely affected by counterfeits in recent years. Like other successful brands, it is also subjected to the ongoing technical progress of counterfeiters. Many of the brand's models will need to be opened in order to check the movement, and in some cases even that will not ensure rapid identification which will require the help of an expert, as you will see in certain cases.

ORIGINAL BIG PILOT POWER RESERVE

FAKE BIG PILOT POWER RESERVE

Here's another model featuring frighteningly good workmanship. Fortunately, even though one can clearly see the "effort" that has been devoted to the movement, one can also soon see that it is not an original calibre, that the balance-wheel is similar but not identical at all, and finally, that the IWC seal on the latter is indented rather than raised. All these differences will reassure connoisseurs of real watches.

ORIGINAL PILOT

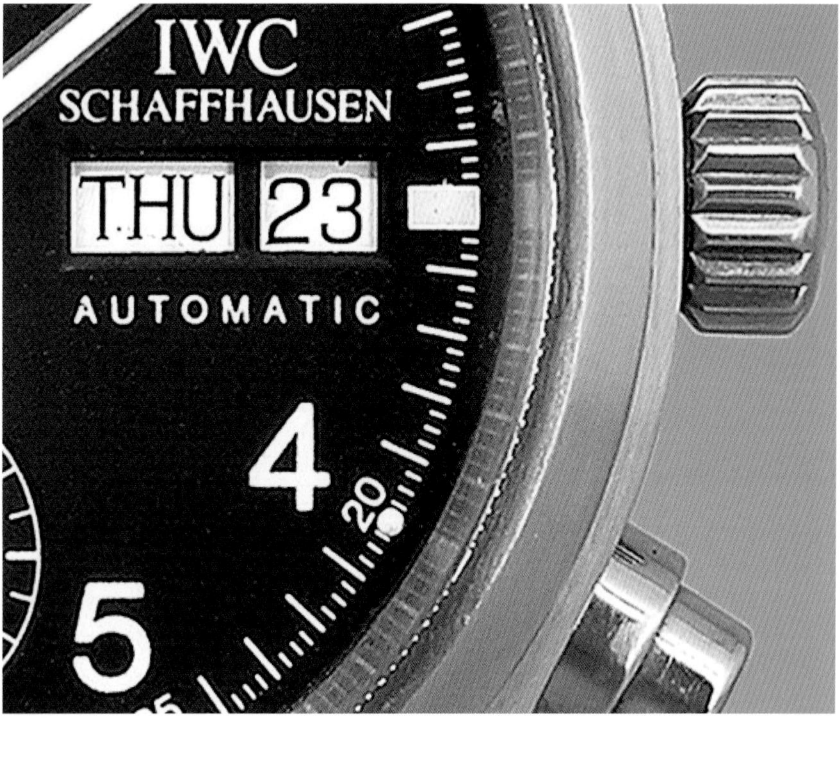

FAKE PILOT

This is another model that might have been scarily close to the original, but the hoax is quickly exposed by opening the watch and a connoisseur wishing to acquire this model will be reassured that it's best to leave this watch with its would-be seller.

ORIGINAL PILOT TOP GUN

FAKE PILOT TOP GUN

All the details have been carefully imitated on this model, and even though an informed connoisseur will detect the mistaken size of the central chronograph seconds hand (which is smaller on the fake than on the original), you will need to have the original in hand in order to identify the fake. A model that should be submitted to an expert before you decide to buy one.

ORIGINAL INGENIEUR CHRONOGRAPH

FAKE INGENIEUR CHRONOGRAPH

So as not to discourage the most passionate collectors among you, here's a model that can be legitimately described as a "cheap imitation". Even on the photo, the finishing is obviously of poor quality, with rounded edges, a poorly finished case-back, steel instead of titanium, etc.

ORIGINAL INGENIEUR TITANIUM

FAKE INGENIEUR TITANIUM

The counterfeiters have gone so far as to make this watch from good-quality titanium. However, the rest of it is a failure: it has an incorrect date display font and a cheap imitation ETA movement. This is another model that is nonetheless worth opening up when considering a purchase.

ORIGINAL PORTUGUESE POWER RESERVE

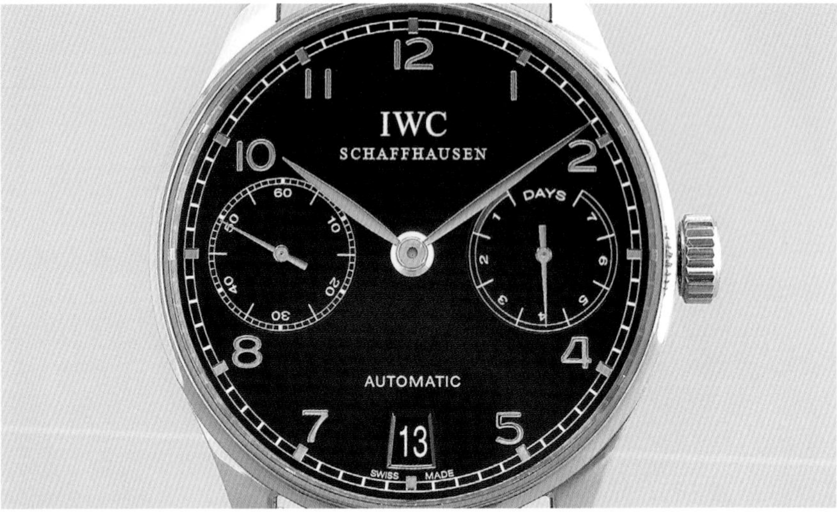

FAKE PORTUGUESE POWER RESERVE

Same comment as for the "Big Pilot – Power Reserve" model (see previous pages).

ORIGINAL PORTUGUESE

FAKE PORTUGUESE

IWC's Portuguese is the brand's most widely copied model. This fake is an extremely poor-quality model equipped with a badly made Asian movement. Such is unfortunately not the case for all models (see the following page).

ORIGINAL PORTUGUESE F.A. JONES

FAKE PORTUGUESE F.A. JONES

This is a very worrying model. Despite certain differences on the movement, such as the central screw at the centre of the large gear train on the fake, which does not appear on the original, and certain other obvious details, it shows many signs of the considerable effort expended on copying an original movement that is both finely crafted and definitely out of the ordinary, thus vividly illustrating the ongoing progress being made by the counterfeiters.

ORIGINAL NAUTILUS JUMBO POWER RESERVE

FAKE NAUTILUS JUMBO POWER RESERVE

Even though the movements and the quality workmanship of this prestigious brand are scarcely likely to be realistically imitated, I nonetheless wanted to include this particular model in order to show how far counterfeiters are prepared to go in order to turn a profit.

ORIGINAL GRANDE CHRONOMASTER OPEN POWER RESERVE

FAKE GRANDE CHRONOMASTER OPEN POWER RESERVE

The brand with the star symbol over its logo is not widely copied, which is strange when one considers its success and the demand for its products. The fake models are often poorly made, such as this Open model with a dial showing an inverted power-reserve display and an El Primero calibre replaced by an extremely bad copy of a Lemania movement. No particular cause for concern here...

Part 4

Counterfeits today and the future of "fakes"

We have just taken a look at what is available on the counterfeit market, mainly on the internet.

This market is mainly at aimed at the public at large and is entirely operated by the world's largest criminal organizations. This market generates sales worth billions of euros and is unfortunately one of the most sought-after types of criminal activity because the stakes are not so high in terms of potential punishment.

This market can be divided into three parts: distribution of mass-consumer fakes; very well-made models (less widely distributed); and the market run by forgerers capable of producing what are often called "genuine fakes".

This chapter presents these products in more detail.

Cottage-industry type production

It's easy to understand how countries such as China manage to produce fairly well-made watches at ridiculously low prices. Extremely cheap labour, coupled with well-organized assembly and distribution networks, enable smooth mass production. Meanwhile, other countries have become specialized in creating "cottage-industry" fakes.

This is particularly true in certain countries of the former Soviet Union or in South America, where one can find 100% fake models, as well as others based on a real watch and hand-finished by combining other parts from other original or fake models. While this kind of product may satisfy some buyers not too concerned about quality, such is rarely the case for collectors and other connoisseurs of extremely rare or vintage watches.

It is not unusual to find old Patek Philippe, Omega, Vacheron Constantin or even Breguet watches, along with military watches, a big favourite with connoisseurs. The problem is that it is almost impossible to identify this type of watch unless you're an expert in the field.

Some might be tempted to say that a collector who acquires a rare piece generally is an expert and as such should be capable of identifying a watch when he is prepared to invest 20,000 euros in the model of his choice – especially since those 20,000 euros, even if passion is the overriding factor, nonetheless represent a well-calculated risk. Nonetheless, there have already been instances where a fake model slips through the net and is sold by a prestigious auction house; these are extreme cases for watches that fetch extreme prices. But even less ambitious collectors face the problem.

© FH 2009

FAKE

Here is an example of a "do-it-yourself" watch. This Submariner 5517 military watch is in fact just a simple Submariner 5513 in disguise. The dial has had a makeover and the hands are fake (the logo is not the right size, the circled "T" is wrong, the 660 has a folding buckle which was never the case for this model and the hour-markers are hand-painted – to mention only the most glaring differences). A collectors' watch that can cost its purchaser dearly: around 20,000 euros for a modified 5513 watch worth around 4,000 euros!

High-quality production

Asian countries equipped with the best machinery are now able to reproduce certain models almost to perfection. This level of production implies a smoothly run production/assembly/distribution chain. While some still think they will find a fake production factory in the middle of China that manufactures the best pieces, they have got it all wrong.

The parts are produced in one place, and then assembled in various other locations before being stamped with the brand name and finally distributed around the world. The operation is masterfully handled by well-organized criminal organizations capable of keeping pace with ever growing demand. The production quality of counterfeits has improved to an alarming extent in recent years and it is not unusual to find models potentially capable of matching the real manufacturer's quality controls – not that they will ever have the chance to

be subjected to them. Some fake movements have now reached an incredible level of similarity.

What can be done in the face of this scourge? Should one just give up the whole idea of buying a watch more cheaply on the internet? That does indeed seem a wise idea unless the model in question is actually handed over personally at a specialist's premises as part of a transaction initiated by correspondence, and accompanied by the presentation box and original documents – or papers as they are usually described. It's certainly preferable to do nothing and to await a less risky transaction – especially when it's just a matter of saving a few hundred or even a mere few dozen euros.

FAKE
METER 400
300
240
EBEL
WED
6
AUTOMATIC
CHRONOMETER
200
180
160
140
130
SWISS
MADE

Here is an extremely high-quality fake. It is practically impossible to identify it without the presentation box and the papers, as well as the bill of sale. This is a real problem in the pre-owned market, especially since many of us enjoy changing watches quite often and are prepared to sell our most recent acquisition in order to buy the next model, or a watch by another brand.

In order to save money, counterfeiters tended to use poor-quality metals for many years, a fact that could facilitate identifying a fake. However, because more and more buyers were prepared to spend over 500 euros on a fake, they soon realized that there was a new market aimed at enthusiasts of higher quality fakes and who don't really care where their watch comes from.

The days when one could simply compare two watches and play the game of "spot the differences" are past. Now it often takes an expert eye.

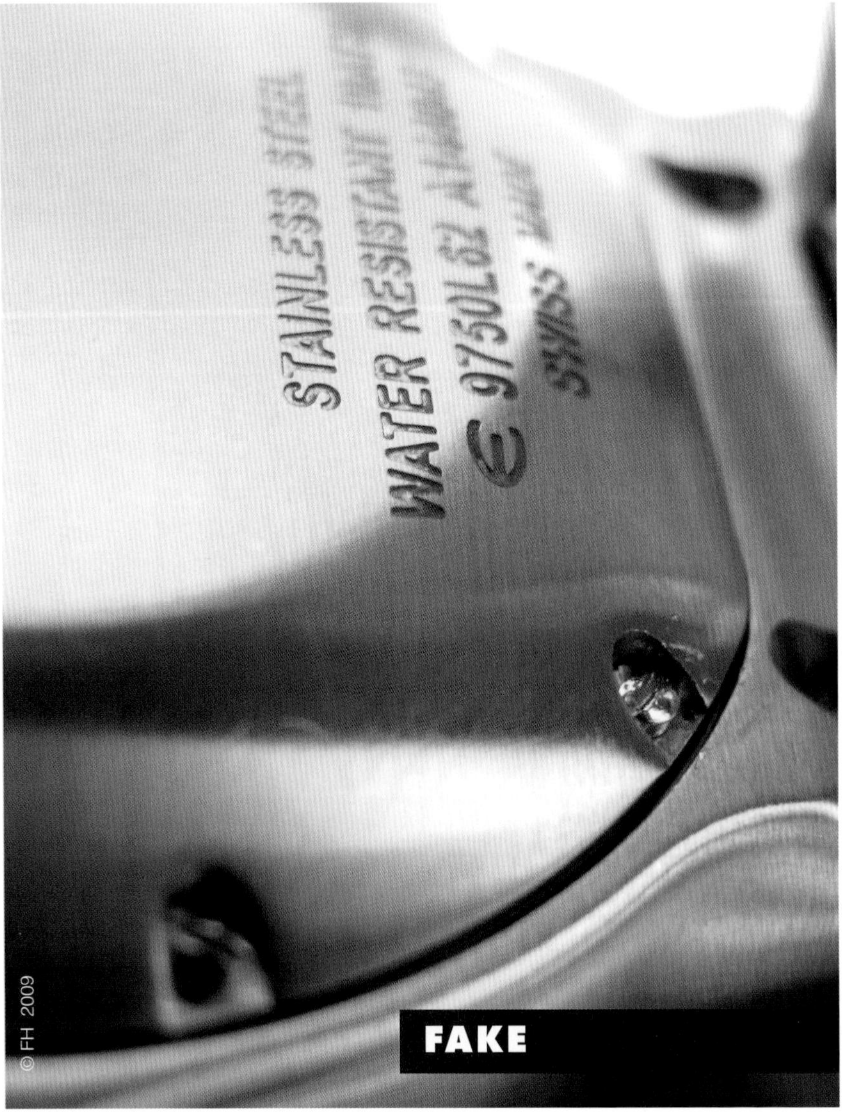

© FH 2009

Watch brands are being increasingly attacked on their standard models, equipped with ETA movements. A watch such as this BR 01-92 by Bell & Ross is one such example. To please devotees of military watches that are normally reserved for the armed forces, Bell & Ross had the idea of producing models for the civilian market, as had been previously done by brands such as Breguet and Auricoste with the famous Type XX model after World War II.

These watches are not *haute horlogerie* models and are thus relatively easy to copy for a manufacturer with the finest equipment. The growing demand for this type of model has given rise to a truly alarming level of production of fake watches, to the understandably great displeasure of the brand and of connoisseurs.

As they continue to push the envelope in their avid pursuit of profits, counterfeiters are targeting all kinds of models, fine-tuning them over the months and trying to reproduce the kind of details that made the original model a genuine high-quality watch. As far as the quality of the materials is concerned, nothing is left to chance in their use of all kinds of metal, rubber, ceramics and 750 (18ct) gold, and they have quickly grasped the fact that there is an extremely lucrative market here. The worldwide economic crisis definitely affected the sales of the major watch brands, but as far as the fake market is concerned, it acted more like a springboard. The watch presented on these two pages is an example of what can currently be produced and sold at a modest price (less than 500 dollars) on the internet.

This is a typical example of what can be achieved in terms of finishing. It is, for example, less expensive to equip a fake with a metal bracelet rather than an exotic leather strap or a rubber strap secured by a groove-type system such as the model pictured here. Nevertheless, the counterfeiters have made an excellent job of it. This is because for an additional cost of around five euros per model, the final sales price will enable them to turn an over 20-fold profit.

The same goes for the calibres equipping fake watches. Two years ago, they were still generally equipped with poor-quality imitation ETA calibres. But the quality has now been considerably improved in this area, and all kinds of finer details are now emerging. We can now find watches equipped with quality movements: milled parts, identical markings, bridges stamped with the brand's logo, recut balance-wheels (mainly for sports models), etc. The movement shown below and the fake Panerai calibre on the two following pages vividly illustrate this trend.

FAKE

FAKE
OFFICINE
PANERAI
17 JEWELS
© FH 2009

Concerned with developing their products, the brands have naturally wished to innovate in terms of materials. This move began with PVD-treated cases, followed by watches equipped with ceramic parts. It took over three years to see fakes equipped with such materials hit the market. But here again, something that was initially an impediment for Asian production is no longer a problem, and one can now find watches that simply could not be found before and were deemed impossible to fake. Here is an example of a fake Hublot Big Bang.

FAKE
© FH 2009

FAKE
HUBLOT
GENEVE
© FH 2009

Haute horlogerie watches are also affected by the fake industry. Even though it is still rare to find truly top-quality fakes of this nature, the race for quality must go on and nobody can afford to rest on their laurels.
Over the past two years, counterfeiters have started to attack brands such as DeWitt and Richard Mille. As far as the latter brand is concerned, the attempts are still laughable – but wasn't that the case two years ago for the fake DeWitt models?

FAKE
DE WITT
CHRONOGRAPH
© FH 2009

FAKE
© FH 2009

Conclusion

The situation is pretty scary, and one can genuinely wonder whether it's still possible to buy a watch without actually seeing it, whether vintage or new. Some enthusiasts who have become "specialists" out of necessity will say that it is still fairly easy to identify a fake. That may be true when it is physically available for identification, but things are different when a seller offers a Panerai Luminor (see the illustrations) at a 40% discount on the retail price and equipped with the movement presented on the previous pages. While common sense might encourage the potential purchaser to let it go, the lure of a good deal could also lead them to think that this might be a "can't miss" opportunity, the kind that only comes once in a lifetime…

FAKE
LUMINOR
MARINA
PANERAI
© FH 2009

FAKE
© FH 2009

"Genuine fakes": two additional models

I am always wary about presenting certain models and one rarely comes across this type of counterfeit. Nonetheless, I wanted to show you the kinds of things that are done, that can be done and that will probably be done in the foreseeable future. This small additional section is mainly intended for fans of collectable watches. The first is a vintage Rolex moon phase model, and the second an all-gold GMT-Master 1675.
For the first one, you will doubtless notice a certain number of rather blatant differences and mistakes, such as the non-original case and a dial featuring some rather obvious discrepancies. The second model, the GMT-Master, is an entirely different matter, and even a specialist, if he doesn't trust his "first impression", might end up with what is known in collector's jargon as a white elephant.

While my personal battle is directed against the criminal organizations that produce fake watches, taking advantage of this flourishing market to fill their pockets with dirty and corrupt money, I also think it is necessary to ensure that unscrupulous sellers stop making money at the expense of genuine watch devotees who wish to perpetuate the tradition of fine mechanical timepieces.

ROLEX
OYSTER PERPETUAL
VIE
ENE
SERPICO Y LAINO

ROLEX
OYSTER PERPETUAL
WED
MAR
SWISS

PATENTED
TRIGGER
ROLEX
PERPETUAL
CHRONOMETER
SWISS MADE
PATENTED

ROLEX
PERPETUAL
SWISS MADE
PATENTED
F 3

VIE
OFFICIALLY CE
SERPICO Y LAINO

ROLEX
OYSTER PERPETUAL
VIE
ENE
OFFICIALLY CERTIFIED
CHRONOMETER
SERPICO Y LAINO

ROLEX
OYSTER PERPETUAL
WE
MAI

ROLEX
OYSTER PERPETUAL

ROLEX
GMT-MASTER
SUPERLATIVE CHRONOMETER
OFFICIALLY CERTIFIED
19

ROLEX
GMT-MASTER
SUPERLATIVE CHRONOMETER
OFFICIALLY CERTIFIED
T SWISS T

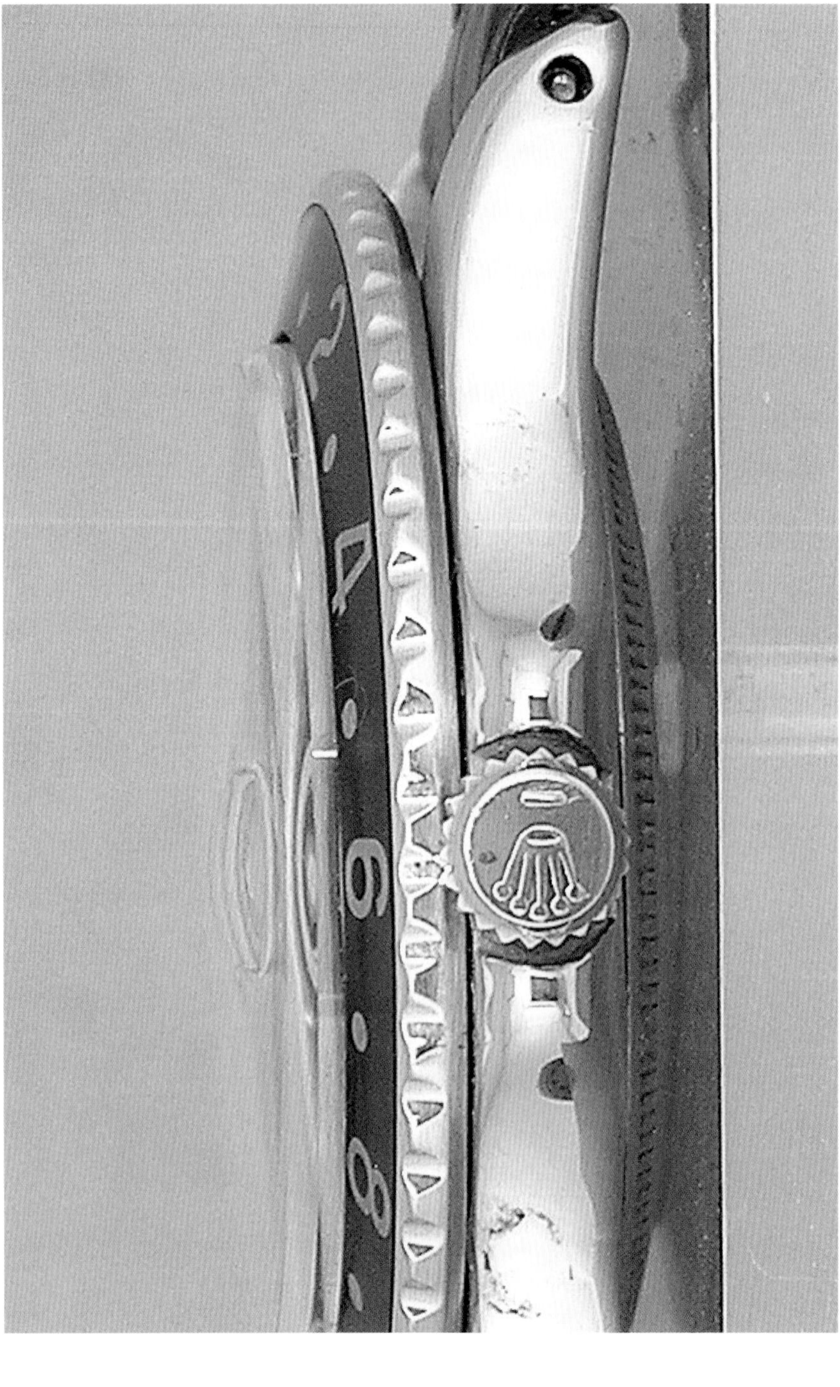

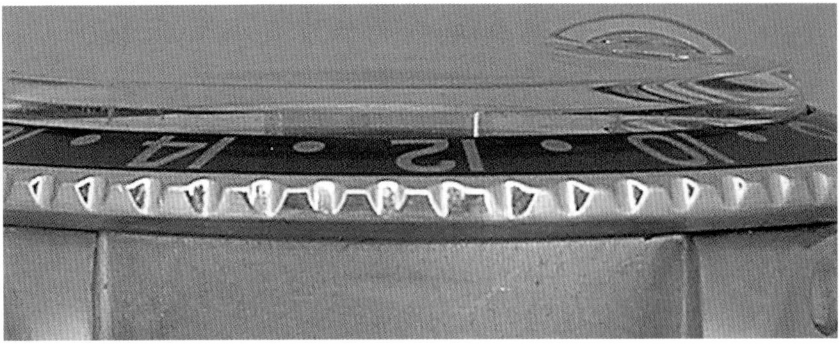

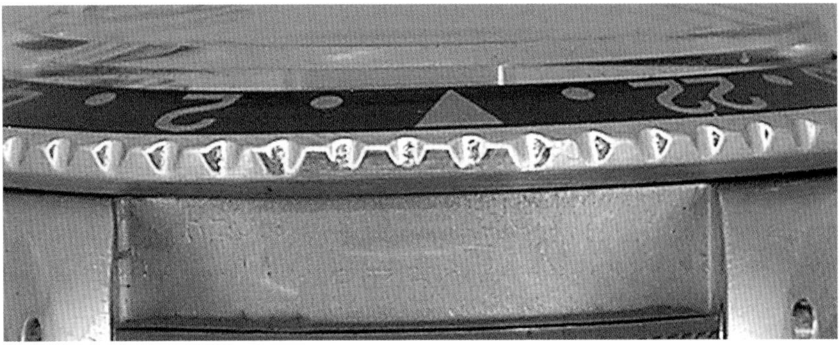

This is a far trickier problem than the moon-phase model. It is impossible to identify it from a photo, because even though the series and model numbers no longer appear on the sides – something that could easily occur with the original (it is after all a 1970s watch that has its own history and may have been erased for a particular reason) – no visual detail enables definite identification. Nonetheless, in comparing the watches, it turned out that if the numbers had indeed been erased, the watch case would be one-third of a millimetre thinner. In fact, not only was this third of a millimetre not missing, but the counterfeit even featured an inter-horn curve one third of a millimetre thicker than the original. Finally, the case-back, which protruded two-thirds of a millimetre from the original, was sunk by one third of a millimetre into the case. The dial, even though very well made on the counterfeit, was a fake. Judge for yourselves – even if that unfortunately implies only by means of the photo...

Part 5

Spare parts and papers

It is fairly common to find watches equipped with fake parts: fake dial, fake case, etc. It is quite easy for a good watchmaker to rebuild a watch using such components, especially for models equipped with ETA movements.
This chapter contains illustrations of authentic parts, mainly dials supplied by the anti-counterfeiting department of the Federation of the Swiss Watch Industry (FH), along with original brand and customer service documents.
This section may be used as a reference basis for identification.

AUDEMARS PIGUET ORIGINALS

BREGUET ORIGINALS

CHOPARD ORIGINALS

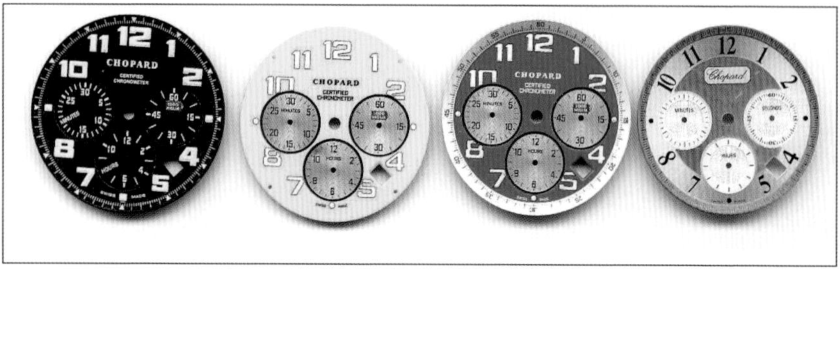

BREITLING ORIGINALS

CARTIER ORIGINALS

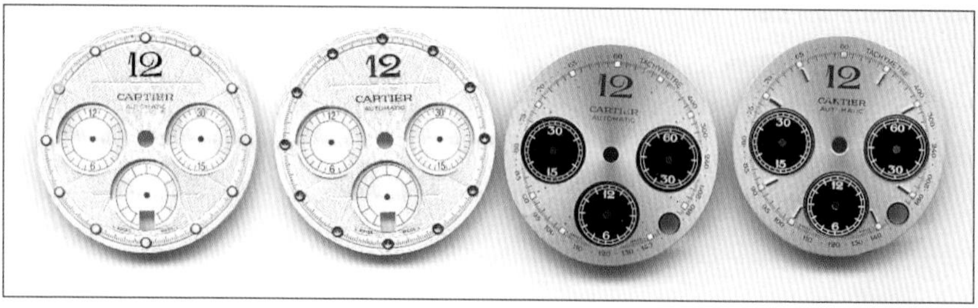

FRANCK MULLER ORIGINALS

GIRARD-PERREGAUX ORIGINALS

IWC ORIGINALS

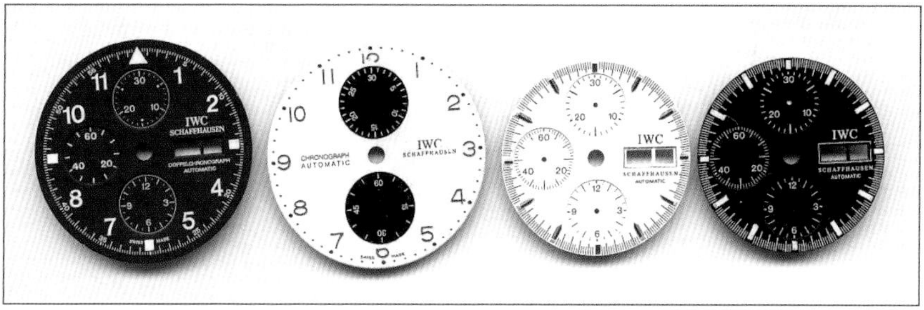

IWC ORIGINALS

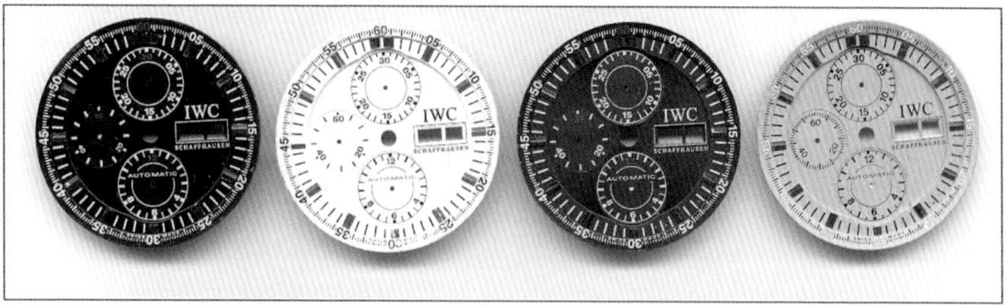

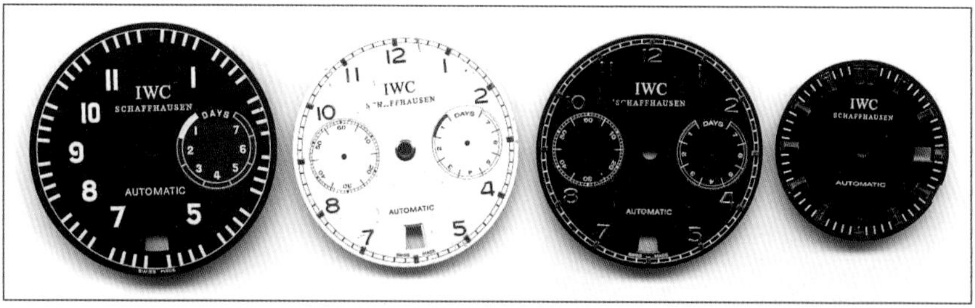

JAEGER-LECOULTRE ORIGINALS

OMEGA ORIGINALS

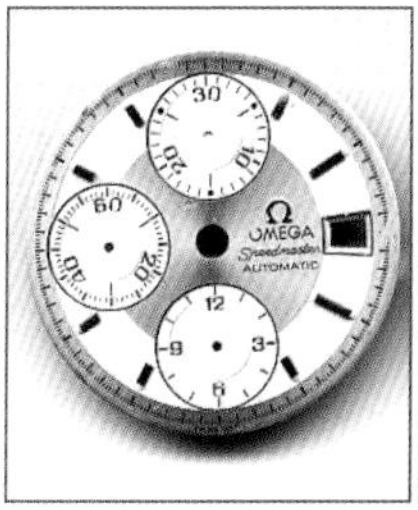

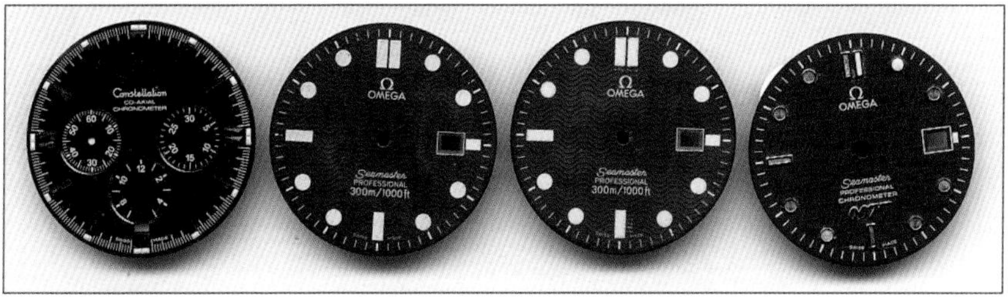

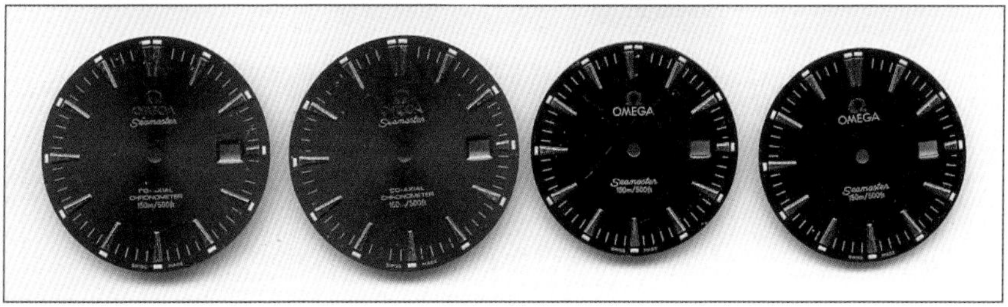

OMEGA ORGINALS

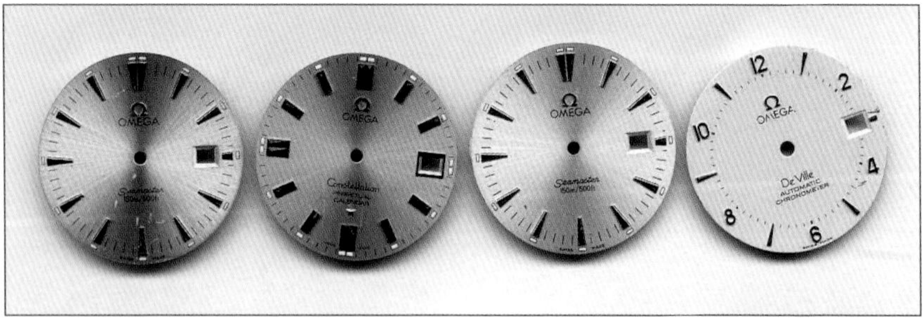

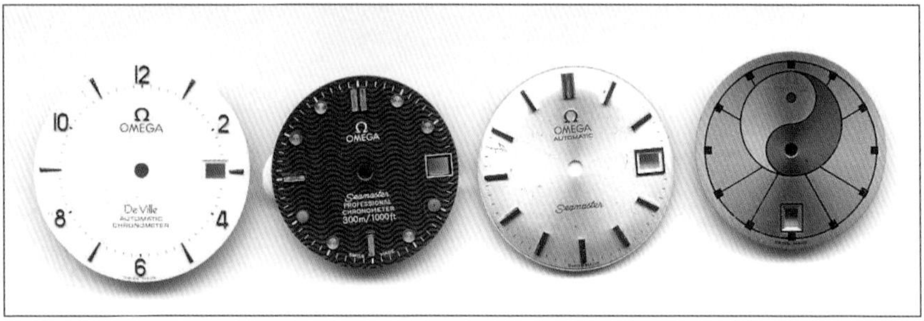

ZENITH ORIGINALS

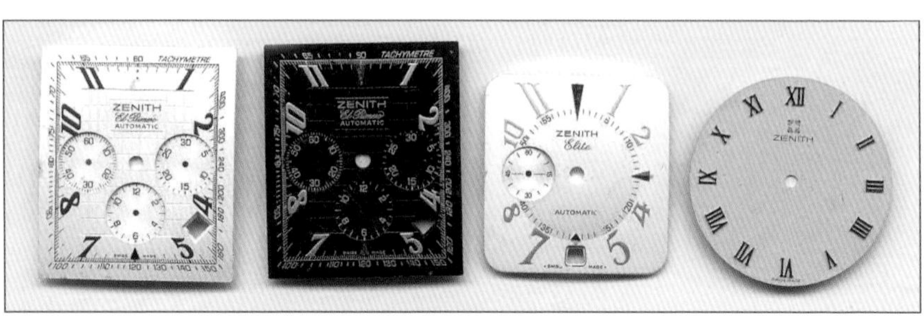

ZENITH ORIGINALS

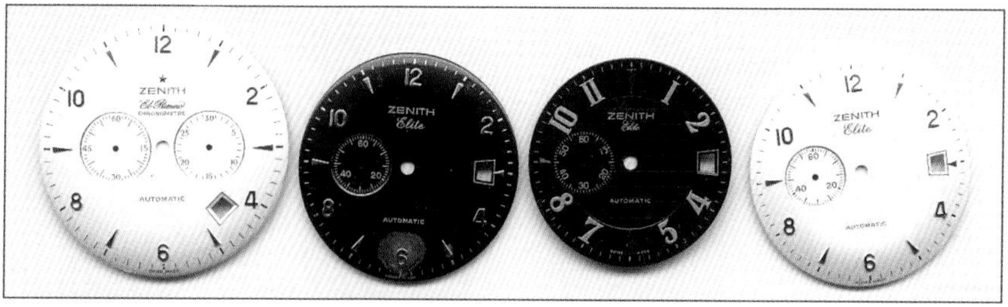

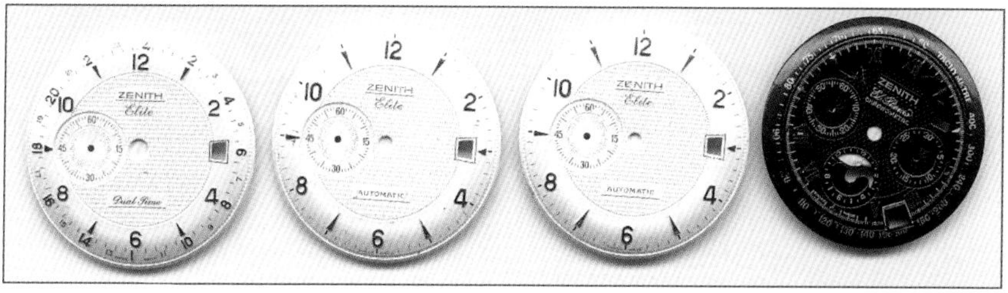

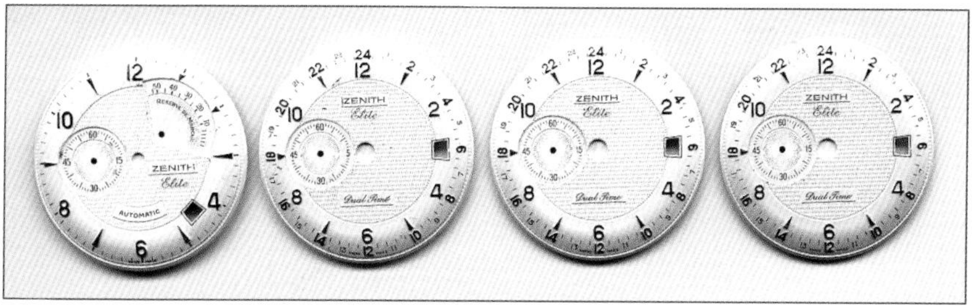

ROLEX ORIGINALS

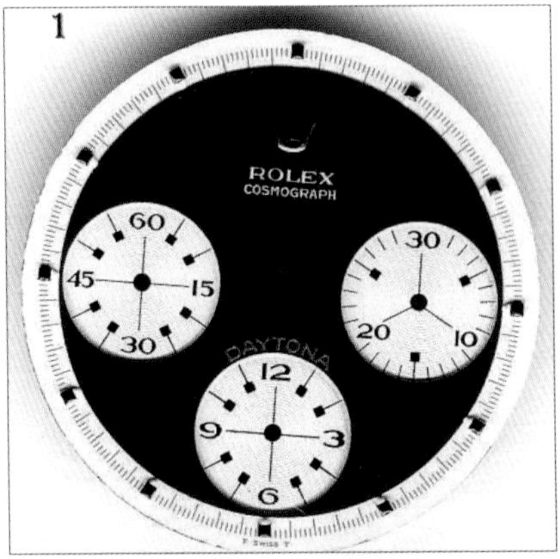

1

9

21

22

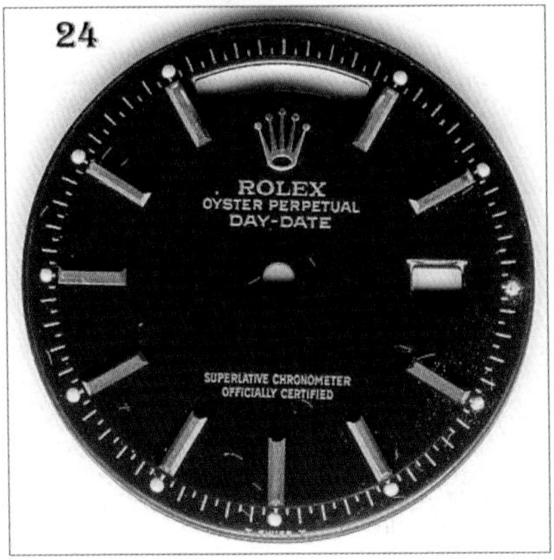

24

14

17

ROLEX
COSMOGRAPH
DAYTONA
T SWISS T

ROLEX
COSMOGRAPH
DAYTONA

ROLEX
COSMOGRAPH
DAYTONA

ROLEX
COSMOGRAPH
DAYTONA
T SWISS T

SINGER

ROLEX
COSMOGRAPH
T SWISS T

When considering buying a watch, be sure to ask for the papers, even if it means the seller has to hunt through the whole house to find them. These papers make all the difference, not only for the purchase itself, but also in terms of the sale and the price of the watch. Original papers and the original box nearly always add to the value of a watch.

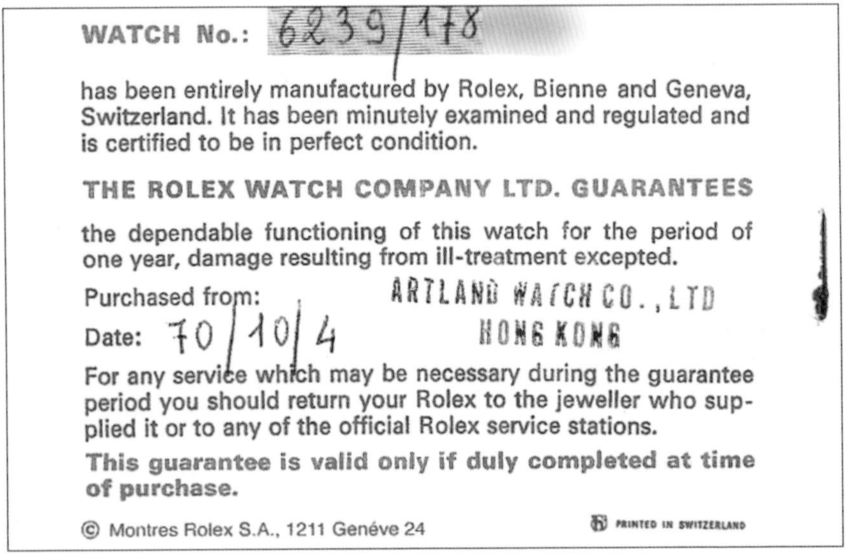

WATCH No.: 6239/178

has been entirely manufactured by Rolex, Bienne and Geneva, Switzerland. It has been minutely examined and regulated and is certified to be in perfect condition.

THE ROLEX WATCH COMPANY LTD. GUARANTEES

the dependable functioning of this watch for the period of one year, damage resulting from ill-treatment excepted.

Purchased from: ARTLAND WATCH CO., LTD

Date: 70/10/4 HONG KONG

For any service which may be necessary during the guarantee period you should return your Rolex to the jeweller who supplied it or to any of the official Rolex service stations.

This guarantee is valid only if duly completed at time of purchase.

© Montres Rolex S.A., 1211 Genéve 24 PRINTED IN SWITZERLAND

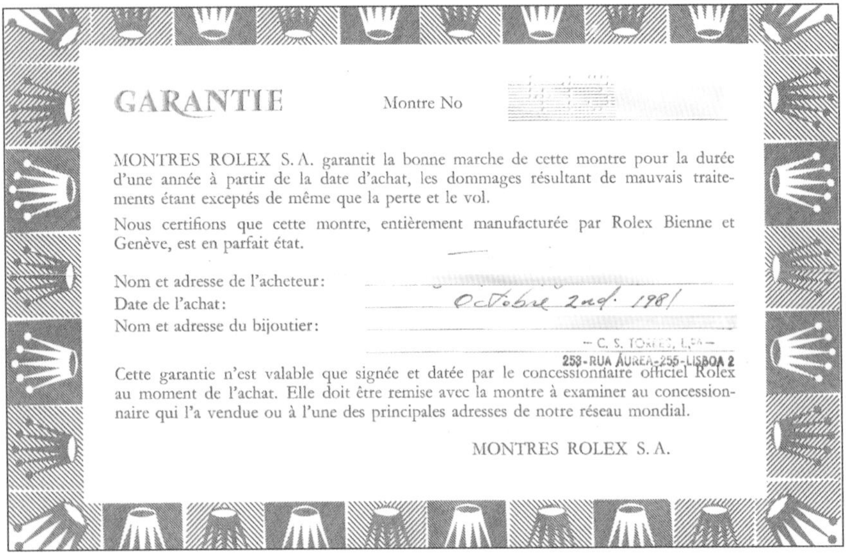

GARANTIE Montre No

MONTRES ROLEX S.A. garantit la bonne marche de cette montre pour la durée d'une année à partir de la date d'achat, les dommages résultant de mauvais traitements étant exceptés de même que la perte et le vol.

Nous certifions que cette montre, entièrement manufacturée par Rolex Bienne et Genève, est en parfait état.

Nom et adresse de l'acheteur:
Date de l'achat: Octobre 2nd. 1981
Nom et adresse du bijoutier:

— C. S. TORRES, L.DA —
253-RUA ÁUREA-255-LISBOA 2

Cette garantie n'est valable que signée et datée par le concessionnaire officiel Rolex au moment de l'achat. Elle doit être remise avec la montre à examiner au concessionnaire qui l'a vendue ou à l'une des principales adresses de notre réseau mondial.

MONTRES ROLEX S.A.

ROLEX

Numéro de Série : 4205208

Garantie de Réparation Internationale

Numéro de Modèle : **1665/0**

Date de la Révision : **05.07.1996**

Cette montre a fait l'objet d'une révision complète dans nos ateliers. Elle est couverte par notre garantie de réparation internationale pour la durée d'une année. Demeurent réservées les exclusions de notre garantie fournie avec les montres neuves.

ROLEX FRANCE

Service Après-Vente

Full One Year Service Warranty

Consumer's Name ______________________

Reference Number X 59135

Watch Serial Number R944570

Date of Service [illegible] 22 19[illegible]

Your Rolex has been thoroughly overhauled, freshly oiled and, where necessary, original parts have been replaced. Its performance again conforms with Rolex standards.

In the event of malfunction arising within one year from the Date of Service, Rolex Watch U.S.A., Inc. will cause the defect to be remedied at no cost to the consumer, once the consumer delivers the watch to either (1) the Official Rolex Jeweler from whom it was purchased or (2) Rolex Watch U.S.A., Inc., 665 Fifth Avenue, New York, NY 10022 or (3) any of the official Rolex Service Centers listed.

This warranty does not cover a watch that has been tampered with or mistreated. Mistreatment includes modification of the watch through the addition or substitution of parts or accessories not manufactured by Rolex and may void this warranty.

This waranty gives you specific legal rights and you may also have other rights which vary from state to state.

Please attach this document to any correspondence regarding this Rolex Watch.

ROLEX WATCH U.S.A., INC.

1323R

ROLEX

GARANTIE Chronomètre:

MONTRES ROLEX S. A. garantit la bonne marche de ce chronomètre Oyster pour la durée d'une année à partir de la date d'achat, les dommages résultant de mauvais traitements étant exceptés.
Nous certifions que ce chronomètre, entièrement manufacturé par Rolex Bienne et Genève, est en parfait état.

Nom et adresse de l'acheteur: BOLLA OSCAR ALBERTO.
Date de l'achat: 1-4-75.
Nom et adresse du bijoutier: KELLY E.V. DE TAPIA.

Cette garantie n'est valable que signée et datée par le bijoutier au moment de l'achat. Elle doit être remise avec la montre à examiner au concessionnaire qui l'a vendue ou à l'une des principales adresses de notre réseau mondial.

MONTRES ROLEX S. A.

ATTESTATION DE CHRONOMÈTRE OFFICIEL

Nous certifions que le mouvement de cette Rolex Oyster Perpetual a subi avec succès, pendant quinze jours et quinze nuits, en cinq positions et à trois températures déterminées, tous les contrôles de précision effectués par l'un des sept Bureaux Suisses de Contrôle Officiel de la Marche des Chronomètres. Ce mouvement a ai droit de porter le titre de Chronomètre Suisse Officiellement Contrôlé.
A la suite de ces sévères épreuves, le mouvement et le boîtier ont encore dû passer un dernier et rigoureux examen dans nos propres laboratoires afin d'obtenir le droit de porter le titre de Chronomètre Rolex Oyster Perpetual à Sceau Rouge, titre attesté par les mots «Superlative Chronometer Officially Certified» qui paraissent sur le cadran et par le Sceau Rouge Rolex qui accompagne ce chronomètre.

LABORATOIRES TECHNIQUES ROLEX

OFFICIALLY CERTIFIED SWISS CHRONOMETER

Printed in Switzerland 570. 01. 300

ROLEX

BUREAUX SUISSES
DE CONTRÔLE OFFICIEL DE LA MARCHE DES CHRONOMÈTRES

Schweiz. Institute für amtliche Chronometerprüfungen
Swiss Institutes for official Chronometer tests — Oficinas suizas de control oficial de Cronómetros

Especially good results
Besonders gute Ergebnisse
Résultats particulièrement bons
Resultados particularmente buenos

Epreuves pour montres-bracelet - Prüfungen für Armbanduhren
Pruebas para relojes de pulsera - Trials for Wristlet-watches

Swiss made

ref. 1500

Bulletin de marche
Gangschein
Boletín de marcha
Watch Rate Certificate

No [redacted]

Mouvement / Werk / Máquina / Movement No [redacted]

Genre / Uhrenart / Género de reloj / Type of watch: B

Particularités / Besonderheiten / Particularidades / Watch specialities: Autom. sec. au centre

Diamètre du mouvement mm / Werkdurchmesser mm / Diámetro de la máquina mm / Diam. of Movement mm: 28,5

Hauteur mm / Höhe mm / Espesor mm / Thickness mm: 5,8

Echappement / Hemmung / Escape / Escapement: ancre

Spiral / Spiralfeder / Espiral / Hairspring: Breguet auto-comp.

Balancier / Unruhe / Volante / Balance: non magnétique

Manufacture des
Montres Rolex S. A.
Bienne-Genève

Jours - Tage Días - Days	Marches journalières Tägliche Gänge Marchas diarias Daily Rates	Variations des marches journalières Differenz der täglichen Gänge Diferencias de las marchas diarias Variations of the Daily Rates	Positions - Lagen - Posiciones - Positions		Températures Temperaturen Temperaturas Temperatures
1.	M_1 + 2		Verticale, 3 heures à gauche Vertical, las 3 a la izquierda	Vertikal, 3 Uhr links Vertical, 3 o'clock left	+ 20° C
2.	M_2 + 2	V_1 0	"	"	"
3.	M_3 + 5		Verticale, 3 heures en haut Vertical, las 3 arriba	Vertikal, 3 Uhr oben Vertical, 3 o'clock up	"
4.	M_4 + 2	V_3 3	"	"	"
5.	M_5 + 1		Verticale, 3 heures en bas Vertical, las 3 abajo	Vertikal, 3 Uhr unten Vertical, 3 o'clock down	"
6.	M_6 + 1	V_5 0	"	"	"
7.	M_7 + 5		Horizontale, cadran en bas Horizontal, esfera abajo	Horizontal, Zifferblatt unten Horizontal, Dial down	"
8.	M_8 + 2	V_7 3	"	"	"
9.	M_9 + 5		Horizontale, cadran en haut Horizontal, esfera arriba	Horizontal, Zifferblatt oben Horizontal, Dial up	"
10.	M_{10} + 3	V_9 2	"	"	"
11.	M_{11} + 6		"	"	+ 4° C
12.	M_{12} + 4		"	"	+ 20° C
13.	M_{13} + 2		"	"	+ 36° C
14.	M_{14} + 3		Verticale, 3 heures à gauche Vertical, las 3 a la izquierda	Vertikal, 3 Uhr links Vertical, 3 o'clock left	+ 20° C
15.	M_{15} + 2		"	"	+ 20° C

Date de la fin des épreuves: [illegible]

Résultats - Ergebnisse - Resultados - Summary

Marche journalière moyenne dans les différentes positions / Mittlerer täglicher Gang in den verschiedenen Lagen / Marcha diaria media en las distintas posiciones / Mean daily rate in the different positions . . . . +2,8

Variation moyenne / Mittlere Gangabweichung / Diferencia media / Mean variation 1,6

Plus grande variation / Größte Abweichung / Máxima diferencia / Maximum variation 3,0

Différence du plat au pendu / Differenz zwischen liegend und hängend / Diferencia entre las posiciones horizontal y vertical / Difference between flat and hanging positions . . . .

Plus grande différence entre la marche journalière moyenne et l'une des marches dans les 5 positions / Größte Differenz zwischen dem mittleren täglichen Gang und einem der Gänge / Máxima diferencia entre la marcha diaria media y una de las marchas en las cinco posiciones / Greatest difference between the mean daily rate and any individual rate 2,2

Variation par degré centigrade / Gangabweichung pro Grad Celsius / Diferencia por grado centigrado / Variation of rate per 1° centigrade . . . . −0,12

Erreur secondaire / Sekundäre Kompensationsfehler / Error secundario / Secondary error . . . .

Toutes les valeurs indiquées sont en secondes
Alle Werte sind in Sekunden ausgedrückt
The values are indicated in seconds
Todos los valores están indicados en segundos

WE CERTIFY	NOUS CERTIFIONS	WIR BESTÄTIGEN,
that this chronometer has been submitted to a final test in our workshops and that its performance was found to be in accordance with this Official Certificate.	que ce chronomètre a subi un ultime contrôle dans nos ateliers et que sa précision est conforme à ce Bulletin Officiel.	dass dieser Chronometer in unseren Werkstätten nochmals einer genauen Prüfung unterzogen wurde, und dass seine Präzision diesem offiziellen Gangschein entspricht.
THE ROLEX WATCH COMPANY, GENEVA	MONTRES ROLEX S.A., GENÈVE	ROLEX-UHREN AG., GENF

PATEK PHILIPPE

PATEK PHILIPPE
GENEVE

Certificat d'Origine
Certificate of Origin

Nous certifions que la montre
We certify that the watch

Référence: [redacted]
Mouvement: [redacted]
Calibre: [redacted]

a été construite et réglée aux diverses températures et positions dans nos ateliers de Genève.
was manufactured, and adjusted at various temperatures and positions, in our Geneva workshops.

Rubis / *Movement jewels:* 31 R
Cadran / *Dial:* ARGENTE - HEURES RELIEF OR-ANG

Boîtier / *Case:* Platine
Bracelet / *Bracelet:* CUIR
Pierres / *Gem stones:*

Nom et adresse du propriétaire / *Name and address of owner:*

Nom, adresse et timbre du concessionnaire agréé Patek Philippe:
Name, address and stamp of authorized Patek Philippe retailer:

PATEK PHILIPPE S.A.

Date de la vente / *Date of purchase:*

PSSS 100208

PRÉSIDENT

Ce certificat n'est valable que si la date de vente est inscrite et que si la montre a été acquise auprès du concessionnaire agréé Patek Philippe dont le nom figure ci-dessus.

This certificate will be valid only if dated and if the watch was sold to the consumer by the authorized Patek Philippe retailer whose name appears hereon.

Remarques importantes au verso / *Important notes overleaf*

Printed in Switzerland / 10'000 / [illegible]

FRANCK MULLER

FRANCK MULLER
GENEVE

Certificat d'Origine et de Garantie

Certificate of Origin and Warranty

Nous certifions que la montre / We certify that the watch

Référence / Reference : ....

Matière / Material : or jaune 18 cts

Boîtier N° / Case N°: ....

Pierres / Gem stones : ——

a été terminée à la main et réglée aux diverses températures et positions dans nos ateliers de Genthod-Genève.

was hand-finished and adjusted at various temperatures and positions in our Genthod-Geneva workshops.

Votre montre est garantie contre toute défectuosité ou vice de fabrication pendant une année.

Your watch ensures a warranty against any manufacturing defect, for one year from the date of purchase.

Nom, adresse et timbre du concessionnaire agréé Franck Muller :
Name, address and stamp of authorised Franck Muller dealer :

....

Date de vente / Date of purchase : 22 janvier 2002

Signature :

Edouard Nahum
Joallier - Créateur - Horloger
20, av. Franklin Roosevelt
75008 - PARIS
Tél : 01 53 96 06 06 - Fax : 01 53 96 06 08

Stamp of agent :

Ce certificat n'est valable que s'il est muni du timbre de l'agent officiel Franck Muller et de la date de vente.

This certificate is valid only when signed and dated by an officially appointed Franck Muller agent.

Conclusion

This work does not claim to be the only reference work on counterfeit watches. The primary asset in this field is a personal passion for timepieces. After a number of years spent collecting and looking at watches, some of us have become "specialists" or "informed connoisseurs". The term is not important, but what counts is that we have become capable of identifying a watch, if only by its finishing details.

This book has been written to help you to do the same, to share this passion with you and to enable you to benefit from hours of work and research.

The first volume was a success and I hope you will be satisfied with the second one and trust it will achieve its goal of providing you with further information and knowledge.

It's a true pleasure for me to share my passion with you.

Fabrice Guéroux

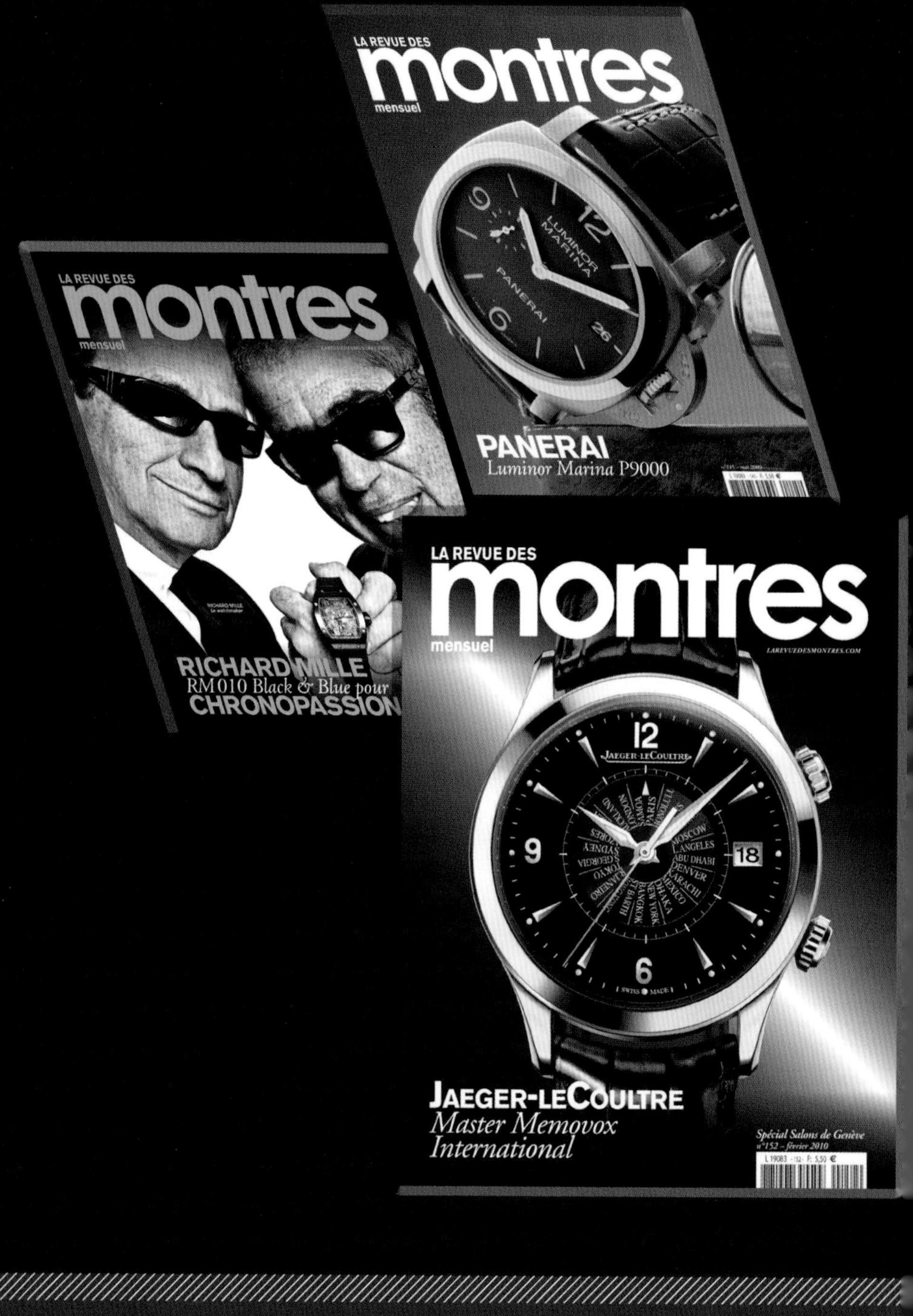

Le mensuel horloger

VIRTUAL IMMERSION IN THE WORLD OF WATCHMAKING
·28·30 1·3·5·
THEWATCHAVENUE.COM
BY EDITIONS TEMPS INTERNATIONAL